FLOYD CLYMER'S MOTORCYCLIST'S LIBRARY

The Book of the
TRIUMPH TWINS

A COMPREHENSIVE AND PRACTICAL GUIDE TO THE PROPER HANDLING AND MAINTENANCE OF 1945-59 TWIN-CYLINDER TOURING MODELS, WITH SOME USEFUL ADVICE TO OWNERS OF 1937-9 TWINS

BY

W. C. HAYCRAFT, F.R.S.A.

ANNOUNCEMENT

By special arrangement with the original publishers of this book, Sir Isaac Pitman & Son, Ltd., of London, England, we have secured the exclusive publishing rights for this book, as well as all others in THE MOTORCYCLIST'S LIBRARY.

Included in THE MOTORCYCLIST'S LIBRARY are complete instruction manuals covering the care and operation of respective motorcycles and engines; valuable data on speed tuning, and thrilling accounts of motorcycle race events. See listing of available titles elsewhere in this edition.

We consider it a privilege to be able to offer so many fine titles to our customers.

FLOYD CLYMER
Publisher of Books Pertaining to Automobiles and Motorcycles
2125 W. PICO ST.   LOS ANGELES 6, CALIF.

INTRODUCTION

Welcome to the world of digital publishing ~ the book you now hold in your hand, while unchanged from the original edition, was printed using the latest state of the art digital technology. The advent of print-on-demand has forever changed the publishing process, never has information been so accessible and it is our hope that this book serves your informational needs for years to come. If this is your first exposure to digital publishing, we hope that you are pleased with the results. Many more titles of interest to the classic automobile and motorcycle enthusiast, collector and restorer are available via our website at www.VelocePress.com. We hope that you find this title as interesting as we do.

NOTE FROM THE PUBLISHER

The information presented is true and complete to the best of our knowledge. All recommendations are made without any guarantees on the part of the author or the publisher, who also disclaim all liability incurred with the use of this information.

TRADEMARKS

We recognize that some words, model names and designations, for example, mentioned herein are the property of the trademark holder. We use them for identification purposes only. This is not an official publication.

INFORMATION ON THE USE OF THIS PUBLICATION

This manual is an invaluable resource for the classic motorcycle enthusiast and a "must have" for owners interested in performing their own maintenance. However, in today's information age we are constantly subject to changes in common practice, new technology, availability of improved materials and increased awareness of chemical toxicity. As such, it is advised that the user consult with an experienced professional prior to undertaking any procedure described herein. While every care has been taken to ensure correctness of information, it is obviously not possible to guarantee complete freedom from errors or omissions or to accept liability arising from such errors or omissions. Therefore, any individual that uses the information contained within, or elects to perform or participate in do-it-yourself repairs or modifications acknowledges that there is a risk factor involved and that the publisher or its associates cannot be held responsible for personal injury or property damage resulting from the use of the information or the outcome of such procedures.

WARNING!

One final word of advice, this publication is intended to be used as a reference guide, and when in doubt the reader should consult with a qualified technician.

PREFACE

Triumph twin-cylinder motor-cycles have earned a well deserved popularity for good performance, good looks, reliability, and economical running. Although detail modifications in design have been made during the past few years, basic design, especially of the power units, has not undergone radical alteration (except on Models 3TA and 5TA). A very efficient type of engine does not require to be repeatedly altered, and this is obviously of considerable benefit to the buying public both in regard to the purchase of new or second-hand machines and the obtaining of spare parts.

The present edition of this handbook (rewritten throughout) gives essential maintenance instructions for 1945–59 twin-cylinder Triumphs of 350 c.c., 500 c.c., and 650 c.c. capacity. These models include Models 5T, 5TA, 3TA, 3T de luxe, T100, T110, TR5, TR6, and T120. Single-cylinder Triumph models are not covered, but much advice is also given about 1937–9 twins.

The purpose of this handbook is to assist you to obtain the maximum pleasure, mileage, m.p.g., and m.p.h. from your new or second-hand Triumph Twin and to keep its depreciation down to the minimum.

If you have not previously handled a Triumph, turn direct to Chapter I, which deals with preliminaries, starting up, and driving. Space does not permit of the legal aspect of driving being dealt with and where the holder of a provisional licence is concerned, it is vital that he should study the *Highway Code* most carefully and do all in his power to avoid accidents. Always remember that there are plenty of bad drivers on the road and that the annual registration figures and road casualties are increasing at an alarming rate. Do not forget to wear a crash helmet!

In conclusion I thank the Triumph Engineering Company, Ltd., of Meriden Works, Allesley, Coventry, for their generous assistance in regard to technical data, and for kindly permitting various Triumph copyright illustrations to be reproduced. Various accessory firms are also thanked for their helpful co-operation.

W. C. H.

CONTENTS

PAGE

CHAP.
I. Handling a Triumph 1
Getting on the road—The controls—Starting—Riding hints

II. Correct Carburation 11
Amal standard carburettor—Amal "Monobloc" carburettor—Tuning the carburettor—Amal carburettor maintenance—The air filter—The S.U. M.C.2 carburettor—Petrol tap adjustment

III. Triumph Lubrication 28
Engine lubrication system—Lubricating engine—The motorcycle parts—Changing the oil—Recommended lubricants

IV. Lighting and Ignition Systems 44
The Lucas dynamo—The Lucas magneto—Lucas RM14 and RM15 A.C. lighting and ignition—Lucas lamps (1945–59 models)—Battery maintenance—The horn—Sparking plugs—Checking electrical connexions

V. General Maintenance: The Motor-cycle . . . 68
Cleaning—Forks and steering head—Wheels, brakes, tyres—Chain maintenance—Frame and sidecar hints—The gearbox and clutch

VI. General Maintenance: The Engine 93
Valve clearances—Valve timing—Ignition timing (magneto)—Ignition timing (coil models 5T and 6T)—Ignition timing (coil models 3TA and 5TA)—Decarbonizing and grinding-in valves—The connecting-rod and crankshaft assembly—The twist-grip—Engine removal (1945–59)

Appendix: Summary of Maintenance after Running-in . 127

Index 131

CHAPTER I

HANDLING A TRIUMPH

THOSE who have previously handled other makes of four-stroke motor-cycle should acquire the knack of handling a Triumph almost immediately. But novices should not attempt to ride on the road until they thoroughly understand the layout and use of the various controls.

Getting on the Road. Before you can legally get on the road, you must attend to the following essential preliminaries—

(1) Insure against all *third-party* risks and obtain the vital "certificate of insurance." With a new machine you cannot get this until the machine is licensed, and an insurance "cover note" must be obtained. If you have a valuable machine, you are advised to take out full comprehensive insurance.

(2) Obtain the registration licence and registration book (Form R.F. 1/2*), or renew the licence (Form R.F. 1/A).

(3) Obtain a six-monthly "provisional" or a three-year driving licence (Form D.L.1).

(4) Fit a reliable speedometer if one is not fitted to show within $\pm$ 10 per cent when 30 m.p.h. is being exceeded.

(5) If you carry a pillion-passenger, see that he or she sits *astride* a proper pillion seat securely *fixed* to the machine (all "springers" have dualseats), and that the passenger holds a current three-year driving licence if you are a "learner."

(6) If you are ineligible for a three-year driving licence, attach "L" plates to the front and back of the machine.

(7) If not already provided, fit a red reflector (1½ in. minimum diameter) *vertically* at the rear of the motor-cycle, and in the case of a sidecar outfit an additional red reflector and lamp at the rear of the sidecar and at the same height as on the motor-cycle.

(8) Use an ignition suppression plug if the machine was registered for the first time after 1st July, 1953.

Official forms may be obtained from a money-order post office.

You are not eligible for a three-year driving licence for Group G *unless* you are at least 16 and have complied with one of these conditions—

(*a*) Have held a licence (other than a provisional or Visitor's licence) authorizing the driving of vehicles of the class or description applied for

---

* The Triumph engine number is required on Form R.F. 1/2. It is on the near-side of the crankcase just below the cylinder block flange. All models are taxed at £3 15s. per annum, with £1 5s. extra duty for a sidecar.

within a period of 10 years ending on the date of coming into force of the licence applied for.

(b) Have passed the prescribed driving test (this includes a test passed whilst serving in H.M. Forces) during the said period of 10 years.

Taking over the Machine. The following points should be noted when taking over the machine—
(1) See there is a full supply of oil in the various units.

Carefully check that the oil tank, primary-chain case and gearbox levels are correct (see Chapter III), that the battery is in a charged condition, "topped up" to the correct level and that the battery connexions are secured (see Chapter IV). Check the tyres with a pressure gauge and adjust as necessary (see page 80).

It is advisable after the first 100 miles to re-check the tightness of all nuts and bolts, and again at 500 miles; a precaution necessary owing to the bedding-down of the engine and cycle parts.

(2) See that the riding position makes for comfort and safety; handlebar and controls, saddle, footrest and brake pedal all allow for widely variable adjustments.

Handlebars. Adjust by slackening off the four "U"-bolt nuts and turning the handlebar to the desired position. The TR5 and TRS handlebar is clipped to the top lug by four set-screws; by releasing these the handlebar can be adjusted in a similar way. See that the nuts or set-screws are tightened securely.

Saddle. The twinseat cannot be adjusted for height, but is designed to suit the average rider.

Footrests. The left footrest is located by two pegs; three different positions are available. The right footrest is mounted on a taper and may be placed in any desired position on the rigid-frame models; it is not adjustable on models with the swinging-arm frame. On most recent swinging-arm models neither footrest is adjustable. In the case of models 3TA and 5TA, however, both footrests are mounted on a taper. Each footrest is secured by a bolt and nut. To make an adjustment, loosen the fixing, jar each footrest free of the taper and re-tighten in the best position. Where an adjustment of the two footrests is made it is likely that an adjustment of the rear-brake pedal and gear-change lever positions are subsequently necessary.

Footbrake Pedal. On the rigid-frame models the pedal is adjustable by adjusting the stop screw, which is on the brake-pedal spindle lug. Re-adjust the rear brake after making an adjustment (see Chapter V). On spring-frame models 3TA and 5TA the position of the rear-brake pedal is adjustable to suit the footrest position. To obtain access to the adjustable-stop screw it is necessary to remove the near-side rear panel from the machine.

Gear-change Lever. The gear-change lever is fitted to a serrated shaft.

Slacken off the set-screw and ease the lever off the serrations to re-position it. Replace it in the desired position and tighten up the set-screw.

Control Levers. To suit the rider's preference, the controls can be moved if the clamping screws which secure the level assemblies to the handlebar are slackened. On models 5T, 6T, T100 and T110, the air lever is positioned on the rear frame back-stays below the saddle.

Control Cables—Adjustment Positions. *Throttle Cable.* On all except the earlier model 6T the adjuster is located in the cable approximately 12 in. from the twist-grip. On model 6T the adjustment is made on the right-hand side of the S.U. carburettor.

Air Cable. On models 5T, T100 and T110, adjust the cable-abutment screw in the carburettor top. No adjustment is possible on the earlier model TR5, and no air cable is fitted on the earlier model 6T and models 3TA and 5TA.

Magneto Cable. On models TR5, T100, T110 and T120, raise the rubber sleeve where the cable enters the magneto; the adjuster can be turned after slackening off the lock-nut.

Clutch Cable. Adjustment is made at the lower portion of the cable immediately above the gearbox casing, except on the later models where there is a knurled adjuster nut in the handlebar lever abutment. To reduce the free movement, turn the nut *clockwise*.

Front Brake Cable. An adjustable thumb-nut is located on the anchor plate, except on later models which have a handlebar adjustment.

THE CONTROLS

Controls and Instruments. *Clutch Lever.* This is situated on the left of the handlebar. It should not be operated when the machine is in motion except to change gear and when stopping.

Front Brake Lever. This is situated on the right of the handlebar. Only gentle pressure should be applied, and the front brake should be used in conjunction with the rear brake.

Throttle Control. A twist-grip operated by the right hand controls the throttle. Twist towards you to open and away from you to close.

Magneto Control Lever. On the left-hand side of the handlebar on models TR5, TR6, T100, T110, and T120; to advance the spark close the lever anti-clockwise; to retard open the lever clockwise.

Carburettor Air Control Lever. On the right-hand side of the handlebar on models TR5 and TR6; pull clockwise to open the air valve. The Amal carburettor air-control lever on models 5T, 6T, T100 and T110, is on the left-hand side of the frame back-stay immediately at the rear end of the saddle or dualseat. Turn the lever away from the stop to open the air valve. The S.U. carburettor mixture-control lever on model 6T is fitted to the base of the carburettor and connects to the jet. Raise the lever to enrich the fuel mixture, and depress the lever, for normal running, to its lowest point (*see* Chapter II).

Horn Button. On the left of the handlebar; push to operate.

Headlamp Dipper Switch. On the right of the handlebar (combined with the horn-push on later models); depress or raise the lever to operate.

Ignition Cut-out Button. On models TR5 and TR6 on the left of the handlebar; depress it to stop engine running. The Trophy (TR5 and

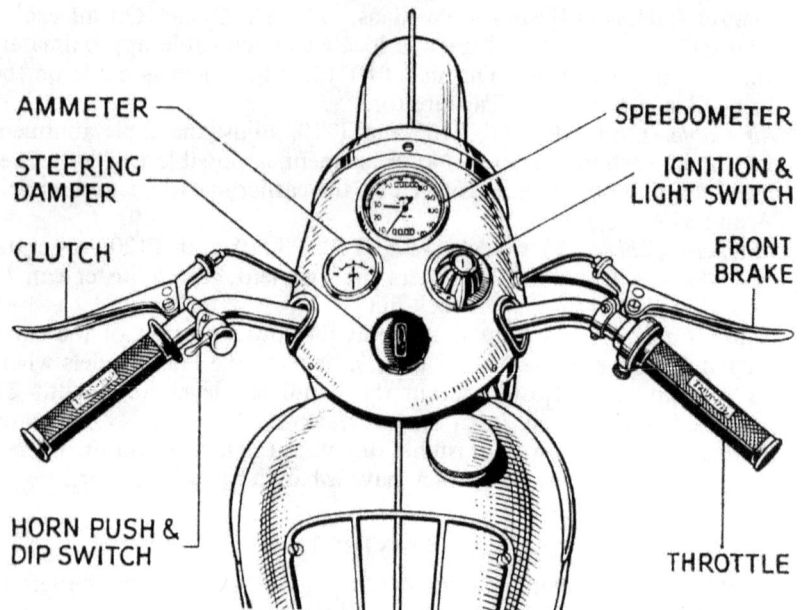

FIG. 1. LAYOUT OF TRIUMPH HANDLEBAR CONTROLS

An air lever (not shown) is provided close to the throttle on models TR5 and TR6, or on models 5T, 6T, T100 and T110 on the near-side of the frame back-stay. On models TR5, TR6, T100, T110 and T120 a magneto control lever (not shown) is fitted near the clutch lever. The slot shown in the centre of the lighting switch for the ignition key applies only to models 5T, 6T, 3TA and 5TA.

TR6) models are fitted with a detachable headlamp in lieu of the nacelle type to enable removal for sporting events. On models T100, T110 and T120 the button is centrally placed in the nacelle. When the button is depressed, ignition to the sparking plugs is "cut-out," by earthing the magneto primary circuit.

Speedometer. The speedometer registers speed, trip and total mileage. Where a combined speedometer and revolution counter is fitted, the central figures indicate in hundreds the engine revolutions in second, third and top gears. Speedometer illumination for night riding is controlled by the main lighting switch. The speedometer on models TR5 and TR6 is mounted on the fork-top lug and its operation is similar. To return the trip position to zero, pull down the flexible cable beneath the nacelle and turn the knob *clockwise*.

Lighting Switch—Models T100, T110, *and* T120. Turn the lever to operate. Switch Positions—

"OFF"	All lights off
"L"	Tail and parking light on
"H"	Tail and headlight on

On models TR5 and TR6 the lighting switch is fitted into the headlamp, but the switch positions are the same.

Lighting and Ignition Switch—Models 5T, 6T, 3TA, *and* 5TA. Turn the lever to operate the lights. Switch positions—

"O"	All lights off
"P"	Tail and parking light on
"H"	Tail and headlight on

Ignition Switch—

"Central" . . .	Ignition off
"IGN" . . .	Ignition on (normal)
"EMG"* . . .	Ignition on (emergency)

Ammeter. This instrument indicates the charging rate of the dynamo or alternator when the engine is running and the amount of discharge when the engine is stopped and the lights are on.

Steering Damper. To increase damping, turn the damper knob clockwise. The damper knob on models TR5 and TR6 is in the same relative position.

Oil-pressure Indicator. This button operates through the oil-pressure release valve positioned in the timing cover. The indicator button *must* protrude at about 30 m.p.h. in top gear to show that oil is being fed to the crankshaft.

Foot Controls. *Footbrake.* This is a flat pedal in front of the left footrest; depress to operate. Apply gently at first and increase pressure as the road speed decreases.

Gear Change. A small lever in front of the right-hand footrest. Move down to select a low gear and up to select a higher gear. The gear selected is shown by a small pointer on many gearboxes. Neutral position is between first and second gears, and the marking "N" on the indicator (where fitted) shows the selected position.

Kickstarter. Located behind the right-hand footrest. All models have the fixed-pedal type, except models TR5 and TR6 which have the folding-pedal type.

* See page 6 before using this switch position.

STARTING

Starting the Engine from Cold (Amal Carburettor). For machines including models 3TA and 5TA, proceed as follows—

Place the gear lever in neutral (between first and second gear).

Turn the petrol tap on.

Lift the clutch lever and operate the kickstarter two or three times. This separates the clutch plates.

If necessary, close the air lever (where fitted) in very cold weather. Move towards the stop to close.

Retard the spark a little by turning the control lever (where fitted) clockwise, i.e. away from the closed position.

Flood the carburettor by means of the tickler on the float bowl until

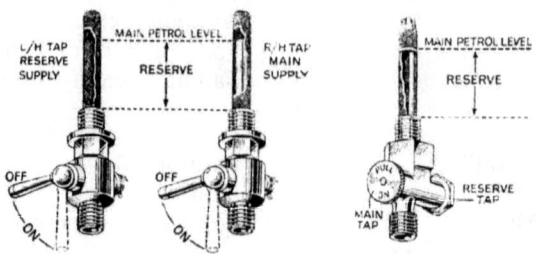

FIG. 2. PETROL TAP POSITIONS

On the left are shown the positions for the L.H. and R.H. taps on models TR5, T100 and T110. On model T120 there is no reserve and both taps must always be used. On the right is shown the petrol tap provided on models 5T, 6T, 3TA and 5TA.

the base of the carburettor is *just* wet. Over-flooding may cause difficult starting.

Turn the engine over until compression is felt on one cylinder. Free the clutch to re-position the kickstarter almost to the horizontal position.

Switch the ignition key to the "IGN" position on models 5T, 3TA, and 5TA.

Turn the twist-grip about one-eighth of a turn to open the throttle slightly. Depress the kickstarter smartly and the engine should fire immediately. Incorrectly set controls may necessitate a second or third kick.

If the battery is flat, a model 5T, 6T, 3TA, or 5TA may fail to start. In this event turn the ignition key to "EMG"—the emergency start position. The engine will fire when the kickstarter is depressed, but as soon as the engine is running the igntion key *must* be returned to the "IGN" position.

As the engine warms up, the air lever (where fitted) should be fully opened as soon as possible, otherwise the mixture strength may be too rich, in which case the oil on the cylinder walls is washed off, with harmful results. Fully advance the ignition lever (where fitted).

Do not allow the engine to idle when cold. To warm the oil quickly and ensure proper circulation, the throttle should be adjusted to a fast tick-over.

Watch the oil-pressure indicator as soon as the engine starts, and remember that the indicator button *must* protrude from the release valve cap. Stop the engine and investigate the failure if the button does not protrude.

When parking turn the petrol taps off.

Starting from Cold (S.U. Carburettor). For earlier machines fitted with an S.U. carburettor, proceed as follows—

Engage neutral gear (N).

Turn on the main petrol tap.

With the clutch lifted, depress the kickstarter two or three times to separate the clutch plates.

To increase the strength of the mixture for a cold start, raise the jet lever on the left-hand side of the carburettor. No definite position can be given, but the rider will quickly find the best lever position. When the engine is warm, put the lever in the lowest position.

Turn the engine over by the kickstarter until compression is felt on one cylinder. By freeing the clutch, re-position the kickstarter pedal almost to the horizontal position.

Turn the key in the centre of the lighting switch to "IGN," open the throttle about one-eighth of a turn, then smartly depress the kickstarter. The engine should fire at once. If not, re-position the jet lever and the throttle. If the engine fails to start after re-setting the controls, the cause may be a flat battery. In this case turn the ignition key to the emergency start position—"EMG." The engine will then fire when the kickstarter is depressed. Return the key to the "IGN" position as soon as the engine is running.

Close the twist-grip to a fast tick-over when the engine starts. The jet lever should be raised just enough to keep the engine running fast and evenly until it is warm and will run with the lever fully depressed.

When parking always turn the petrol taps off.

RIDING HINTS

Running-in. The life of the motor-cycle is reduced considerably if it is handled carelessly during the initial stages of running; hence some space is devoted to a discussion of the subject. To allow the bearing surfaces to harden and bed down, running-in should be carried out progressively. When intelligently and carefully handled, a machine will be faster, mechanically quieter, and will wear longer than the mount of a rider who pays no attention to the finer points which should be considered in running-in.

The fact of paramount importance is that the engine must never be stressed; the best indication of this is the throttle opening. In other words, the engine must not be allowed to labour in the higher gear ratios; changing down to a lower gear certainly causes the engine to rev. faster, but much more easily. For the first 250 miles not more than a quarter throttle opening should be used. After 250 miles increase the throttle opening to one-third.

To enable the rider to judge the throttle opening, it is suggested that a little spot of white paint should be put on the twist-grip rubber, and a spot of black paint on the chromium-plated twist-grip body, in such a position that these coincide when the throttle is closed, or the white spot can be located at a quarter throttle opening, and altered later as an increased opening is desirable. When 500 miles have been covered, the throttle opening can be increased progressively afterwards until full throttle opening is allowable when about 1,200 miles are registered on the speedometer mileage indicator.

It is suggested that the rider of a new Triumph should amble along at a comparatively slow speed throughout the running-in period. Speed bursts are desirable occasionally. If the machine easily reaches, say, 40 m.p.h. with a certain throttle opening, on the first occasion the engine should be throttled down; after a period of slower running 40 m.p.h. may be reached again and held on to for a little longer. By working up gradually in this way the time will come when the first of a few miles at 50 m.p.h. has been arrived at progressively. The same care should be exercised when higher speeds are attained later on during the running-in period. Work up to maximum speed very carefully and hold it for short, but ever-increasing, periods initially. At really high speeds, it is advantageous to close the throttle momentarily at regular intervals during the running-in period, as this allows an increased amount of oil to pass up the cylinder bore. This precaution is not, of course, necessary when the engine has been thoroughly run-in. Summing up: *do not stress the engine.*

Check the various nuts for tightness after 100 miles and again at 500 miles.

Normal Running. The art of driving can only be learned properly by actual demonstration, but the following suggestions are made—

(*a*) A good change can only be made when the road-wheel speed and engine speed are synchronized. In changing up, this is easy, for steady progress with the clutch withdrawal, throttle closing, and gear lever operation allows the engine to slow down to the required revolutions in accordance with the wheel movement. When changing down, accelerate a little after pressing the clutch lever, moving into the lower gear as quickly as possible, with immediate clutch release in both cases.

(*b*) Always drive on the throttle and never on the clutch or the brakes. Keep the fingers right away from the clutch lever and the foot well away from the brake pedal.

(*c*) Use the clutch only for starting, stopping, and gear changing. Never slip the clutch on hills in an attempt to relieve the load on the engine. If it is necessary to stand for any appreciable time with the engine running, engage neutral.

(d) It is always better if hills can be taken at speed, but if this is impossible, owing to conditions or surface, change down early while the machine still has a good speed.

(e) Keep the ignition lever (where fitted) *fully advanced* while riding. When climbing a gradient in top gear, a tendency for knocking can be avoided by temporarily retarding the ignition lever slightly, but remember that retarding the ignition lever reduces power output, and to keep the engine from stalling it is the best practice to change to a lower gear in good time.

In the case of the model T110 when riding at a speed below 40 m.p.h., retard the ignition lever slightly by moving the handlebar lever approximately one-fifth of its travel away from the full advance stop. On this particular machine always run on a high grade fuel.

Stopping. To come to a standstill close the throttle, disengage the clutch and gently apply the foot brake. The engine need not be stopped for a traffic block, but the throttle should be closed sufficiently to allow the engine to "tick over" quietly. The gear lever should be moved to the low gear position as the machine comes to rest so that low gear is engaged in readiness for moving off from stationary. If the engine is stopped, the gear lever should be placed into neutral position.

Steering. Steering a motor-cycle when ridden solo is no more difficult than riding an ordinary bicycle, excepting that one is dealing with a machine that is considerably heavier; hence the need for more care in maintaining absolute control. When riding a sidecar outfit, however, steering is rendered rather different, in that there is always a drag on the cycle in accordance with the precise alignment of the sidecar. When taking a left-hand corner the tendency is for the sidecar to leave the road, but this difficulty is overcome by reducing the speed and leaning well over to the near side.

Some Riding Hints. Having had very considerable experience riding various types of motor-cycles on the road, the author offers the following general hints to Triumph Twin owners, especially to youngsters learning to ride and those who have just passed their driving tests—

(1) Before setting off on a long run, always satisfy yourself that your Triumph *is* thoroughly roadworthy.

(2) Always ride with due consideration for *all* road users, and conform with the law in both letter *and* spirit.

(3) Avoid riding nose to tail. This is a dangerous practice.

(4) Always assume that there *are* bad drivers on your route, and anticipate the unexpected.

(5) Cultivate imagination. Note closely, and where possible foresee, the action of other road users.

(6) Be particularly careful when negotiating cross-roads, especially in suburban areas, where priority roads are often not clearly marked, or not marked at all.

(7) At all times, and especially at night and near hospitals, avoid making excessive and unnecessary noise. This habit gives us a bad name.

(8) In "built-up" areas always keep your speed well within the margin of safety. 30 m.p.h. in the wrong place can be more dangerous than 70 m.p.h. in the right place!

(9) Do not indulge in excessive "stunt" riding. This can bring disaster, though not necessarily for a long time!

(10) Keep at a distance from lady "L" drivers in cars. Some are not mechanically minded, are slow to acquire road sense, and are apt to panic in an emergency. Others are quite good, but it is difficult to identify the two categories. Play for safety by keeping at a safe distance!

CHAPTER II

CORRECT CARBURATION

Some earlier type Triumph twin-cylinder O.H.V. engines have an S.U. M.C.2 type carburettor. An entirely different make and design of carburettor is fitted to all later Triumphs. It is the Amal standard type carburettor fitted to a large number of machines, or else the more recent Amal "Monobloc" carburettor which is specified on all recent and current models. All three types of carburettors are dealt with in this chapter.

AMAL STANDARD CARBURETTOR

An understanding of the working of the standard Amal carburettor is desirable before considering its tuning and maintenance. Referring to Fig. 3 showing a sectional view of the Amal semi-automatic carburettor, *A* is the carburettor body or mixing chamber, the upper part of which has a throttle valve *B*, with taper needle *C* attached by a needle clip. The throttle valve regulates the quantity of mixture supplied to the engine. Passing through the throttle valve is the air valve *D*, independently operated and serving the purpose of obstructing the main air passage for starting and mixture regulation. Fixed to the underside of the mixing chamber by the union nut *E* is the jet block *F*, and interposed between them is a fibre washer to ensure a petrol-tight joint.

On the upper part of the block is the jet-block barrel *H*, forming a clean through-way. Integral with the jet block is the pilot jet *J*, supplied through the passage *K*. The adjustable pilot air intake *L* communicates with a chamber, from which issues the pilot outlet *M* and the by-pass *N*. A throttle stop (*see* Fig. 4) is provided on the mixing chamber, by which the position of the throttle valve for tick-over is regulated independently of the cable adjustment.

The needle jet *O* is screwed in the underside of the jet block, and carries at its bottom end the main jet *P*. Both these jets are removable when the jet plug *Q*, which bolts the mixing chamber and the float chamber together, is removed. The float chamber, which has bottom feed, consists of a cup *R* fed with petrol through union *S*. It contains the float *T* and the needle valve *U* attached by the clip *V*. The float chamber cover *W* has a lock screw *X* for security.

The petrol tap having been turned on, petrol will flow past the needle valve *U* until the quantity of petrol in the chamber *R* is sufficient to raise the float *T*, when the needle valve *U* will prevent a further supply entering the float chamber until some in the chamber has already been used up by

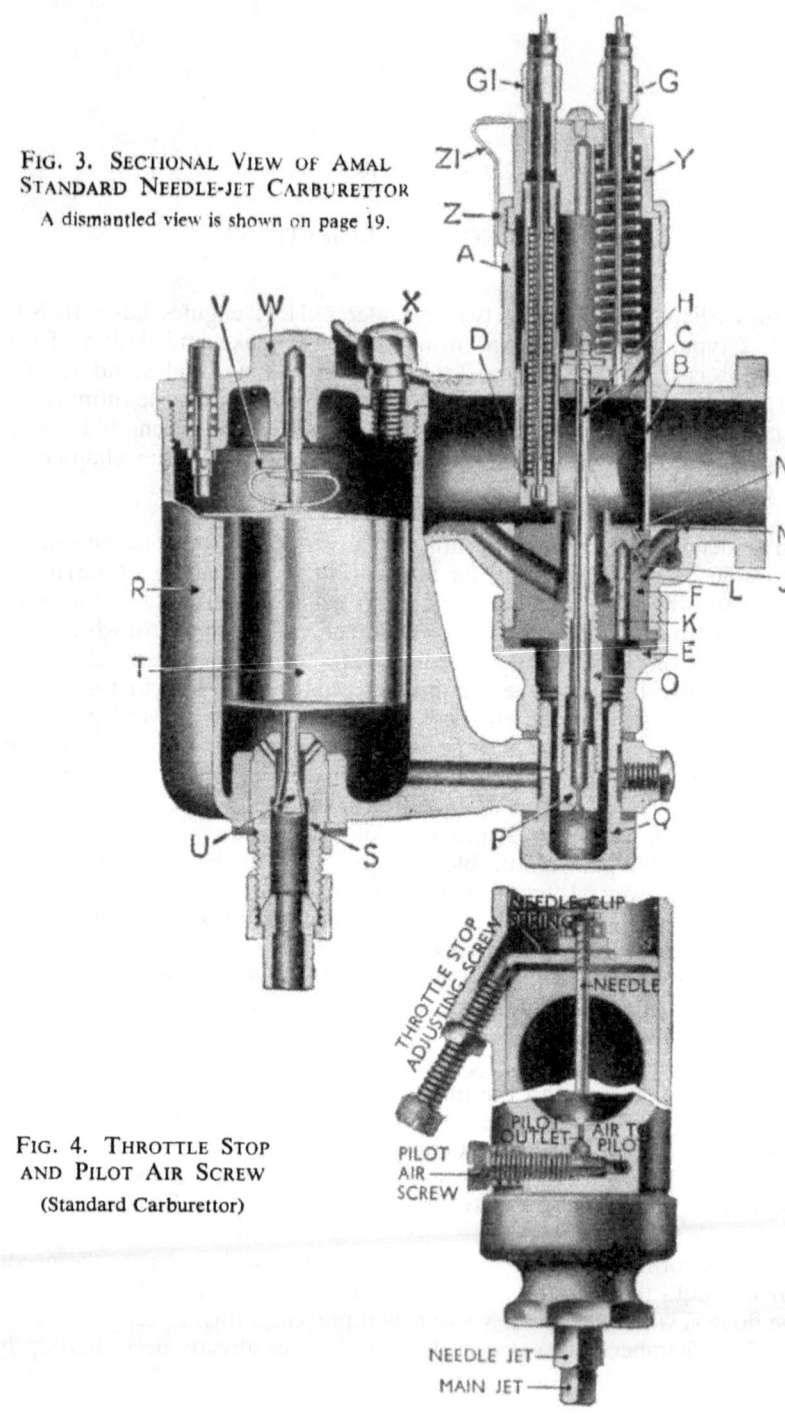

Fig. 3. Sectional View of Amal Standard Needle-Jet Carburettor
A dismantled view is shown on page 19.

Fig. 4. Throttle Stop and Pilot Air Screw
(Standard Carburettor)

the engine. The float chamber having filled to its correct level, the fuel passes along the passages through the diagonal holes in the jet plug Q, when it will be in communication with the main jet P and the pilot feedhole K, the level in the needle and pilot jets being, obviously, the same as that maintained in the float chamber.

Imagine the throttle valve B very slightly open. As the piston descends, a partial vacuum is created in the carburettor, causing a rush of air through the pilot air hole L and drawing fuel from the pilot jet J. The mixture of air and fuel is admitted to the engine through the pilot outlet M. The quantity of mixture capable of being passed by the pilot outlet M is insufficient to run the engine. This mixture also carries excess of fuel. Consequently, before a combustible mixture is admitted, throttle valve B must be slightly raised, admitting further air from the main air-intake.

The farther the throttle valve is opened, the less will be the depression on the outlet M, but, in turn, a higher depression will be created on the by-pass N, and the pilot mixture will flow from this passage as well as from the outlet M.

The mixture supplied by the pilot and by-pass system is supplemented at about one-eighth throttle by fuel from the main jet P, the throttle valve cut-away determining the mixture strength from here to one-quarter throttle. Proceeding up the throttle range, mixture control by the needle position occurs from one-quarter to three-quarters throttle, and from this point the main jet is the only regulation.

The air valve D, which is cable-operated on the standard carburettor, has the effect of obstructing the main through-way and, in consequence, increasing the depression on the main jet, enriching the mixture. Two cable adjusters G, $G1$, are provided.

AMAL "MONOBLOC" CARBURETTOR

The Amal "Monobloc" carburettor specified on all later Triumph Twins differs from the standard type in several respects. But its general functioning is similar. The "Monobloc" design includes: a horizontal float chamber made integral with the carburettor body; a float needle of moulded nylon; a top petrol feed; a needle jet with bleed holes giving two-way compensation; and a detachable pilot jet which can be easily cleaned.

Fig. 5 shows all the essential parts of the instrument. The float chamber (13) and needle (9) maintain a constant level of petrol in the needle jet (14) and the pilot jet (17). The selection by the makers of the appropriate jet sizes and main-bore choke ensures a proper atomizing and proportioning of the petrol and air sucked into the engine.

The air valve (3) is normally kept fully raised, and the throttle valve (24) controlled by the handlebar twist-grip controls the volume of mixture, and therefore the power. At all throttle openings a correct mixture is automatically obtained.

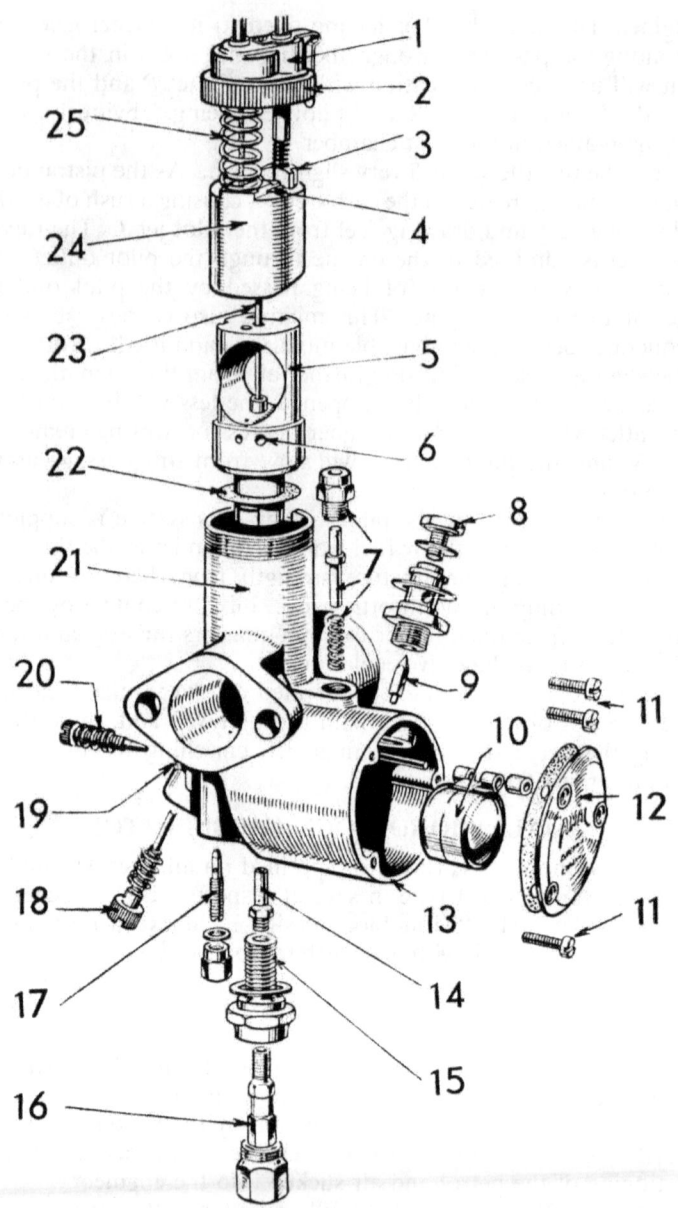

FIG. 5. AMAL "MONOBLOC" CARBURETTOR SHOWN DISMANTLED
By courtesy of B.S.A. Motor Cycles, Ltd.

CORRECT CARBURATION

The "Monobloc" carburettor, like the standard instrument, operates in four stages. When opening the throttle from the fully closed position to one-eighth open (for tick-over) the mixture is supplied by the pilot jet (17), and the strength of the mixture is determined by the setting of the knurled pilot air-adjusting screw (20) which has a coil locking spring to facilitate adjustment. As the throttle is opened slightly farther, the main jet system comes into action, the mixture being augmented by the main jet (16) through the pilot by-pass.

The amount of cut-away on the atmospheric side of the throttle valve regulates the petrol-to-air ratio between one-eighth and one-quarter throttle. The needle jet (14) and the jet needle (23) take over the mixture regulation between one-quarter and three-quarter throttle, and the mixture strength is determined by the relative position of the needle in the clip (4) attached to the throttle valve (24). When the throttle is opened beyond three-quarters, the mixture strength is determined only by the size of the main jet. Note that the main jet (16) does not spray petrol direct into the carburettor mixing-chamber, but discharges through the needle jet into the primary air chamber. From there it enters the main choke through the primary air choke. The latter has a two-way compensating action in conjunction with the "bleed" holes in the needle jet. Pilot and main jet behaviour are not affected by this two-way compensation which governs only acceleration at normal cruising speed.

TUNING THE CARBURETTOR (AMAL STANDARD AND "MONOBLOC" TYPES)

The same tuning instructions apply to the standard and "Monobloc" instruments. Normally it is unwise to interfere with the maker's carburettor setting unless there is a very special reason for doing so. However, it is sometimes desirable to make a slow-running adjustment with the pilot adjusting screw and throttle-stop screw.

To vary the strength of the running mixture, it is necessary to adjust the height of the needle in the throttle valve, or else to fit a larger or smaller size main jet. The condition of the sparking plug provides an

---

KEY TO FIG. 5

1. Mixing-chamber cap
2. Mixing-chamber cap ring
3. Air valve
4. Jet-needle clip
5. Jet block
6. Air passage to pilot jet
7. Tickler assembly
8. Banjo securing-bolt
9. Float needle
10. Float
11. Float-chamber cover screws
12. Float-chamber cover
13. Float chamber
14. Needle jet
15. Main-jet holder
16. Main jet
17. Pilot jet
18. Throttle-stop adjusting screw
19. Jet block locating screw
20. Pilot air-adjusting screw
21. Mixing chamber
22. Fibre seal
23. Jet needle
24. Throttle valve
25. Throttle return-spring

excellent guide to the condition of the mixture. The plug body should be black with no sooty deposits.

Adjustment of Pilot Jet. This should be effected with the engine already warmed up. If the adjustment is appreciably at fault, screw home the pilot air-adjusting screw fully and then unscrew it (usually about two

AMAL CARBURETTOR SETTINGS FOR 1945–59 MODELS

Model	Main Jet	Pilot Jet	Throttle Valve	Needle Jet	Needle Position
5T, 5TA (1945–59)	200	30	376/3½	0·1065	3
TR5, T100 (1945–59)	220	25	376/3½	0·1065	3
6T (1956–9)	270	25	376/3½	0·1065	3
TR6 (1956–9)	250*	25	376/3½	0·1065	3
T110 (1945–59)	250*	25	376/3½	0·1065	3
T120 (1956–9)	240	25	376/3½	0·1065	3
3TA (1958–9)	110	25	375/3½	0·105	3
5TA (1958–9)	160	25	375/3½	0·105	3

* For maximum performance detach the air cleaner rubber hose and fit a No. 270 main jet.

complete turns) until the engine idles at an excessive speed, with the throttle twist-grip closed and the throttle slide abutting the throttle-stop screw. The air lever should be fully open and the ignition lever (where automatic ignition-advance is not provided) should be set to obtain the best slow-running (half to two-thirds advanced).

Loosen the nut (omitted on the "Monobloc" carburettor) securing the throttle-stop screw, and unscrew the latter until the engine slows up and begins to falter. Then screw the pilot air-adjusting screw in or out as required to enable the engine to run regularly and faster. To weaken the mixture, screw the pilot air-adjusting screw *outwards*.

Slowly lower the throttle-stop screw until the engine again commences to falter. Then lock the throttle-stop screw (standard carburettor) with the lock-nut and reset the pilot air-adjusting screw to obtain the best slow-running. If after making this second adjustment the engine ticks over too fast, repeat the adjustment a third time. The combined adjustment sounds complicated but in practice is quite simple. It is important to avoid excessive richness of the slow-running mixture, especially if much riding is done on small throttle openings; if the mixture is too rich, considerable running on the pilot jet will occur while riding, with consequently a high fuel consumption.

Aim at obtaining the best tick-over on a mixture bordering on the weak side. The engine should be on the point of spitting-back. When perfect

CORRECT CARBURATION

slow-running has been obtained, tighten the lock-nut (standard carburettor) on the throttle-stop screw without disturbing the position of the screw.

Obstruction in Pilot Jet. If the adjustment of the pilot jet does not obtain the desired results and the engine will not idle nicely with the throttle almost closed, the air lever fully open, and the ignition lever (where fitted) half to two-thirds advanced, it is possible that the pilot jet is obstructed. The jet passage (on the standard carburettor a duct drilled in the jet block) is very small and can readily become choked.

To gain access to the pilot jet on the standard carburettor (see Fig. 3), remove the jet plug (Q) and the float chamber (R), and then detach the jet block (F) by pushing or tapping it out of the mixing chamber. The pilot jet (J) can then be cleared by blowing through it, or carefully by means of a *very* fine strand of wire.

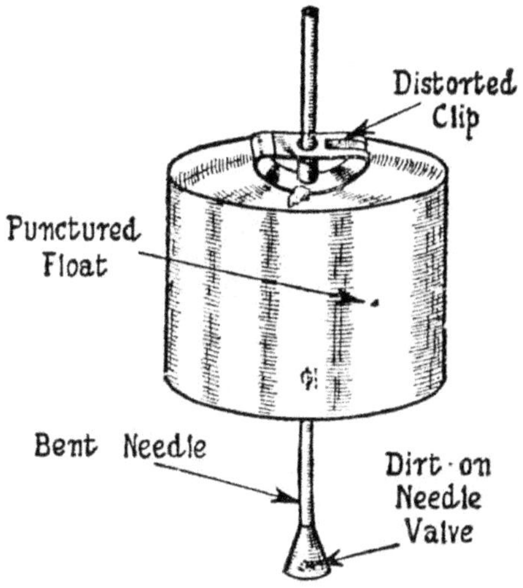

With the "Monobloc" carburettor (see Fig. 5) to remove the pilot jet (17), remove the pilot jet cover-nut and then unscrew the jet itself which should be thoroughly cleaned in petrol and then blown through. See that the air passage (6) to the pilot jet, and also the pilot outlet, are quite clear.

FIG. 6. IF PERSISTENT "FLOODING" OCCURS, LOOK FOR THESE DEFECTS (Standard type carburettor)

Synchronizing Twin Carburettors. On the Bonneville 120 (model T120) the twin Amal carburettors may need to be synchronized in the following manner. Adjust the junction-box h.t. cables so that the free play of the cables is at a minimum. Start the engine and remove one sparking plug lead. Now adjust the pilot air-adjusting screw and throttle-stop screw on the other carburettor until the engine runs smoothly at a normal tick-over speed. Then replace the sparking plug lead and repeat the procedure for the carburettor attached to the cylinder whose sparking plug lead has been replaced.

Bad Slow-running. If it is found impossible to obtain good slow-running by making the pilot jet adjustment as described on page 16, it is probable that some defect other than carburation is responsible for preventing the engine running smoothly at low revolutions. Air leaks or badly-seating valves may weaken the mixture. Defects in the ignition system may also be responsible for poor tick-over. The sparking plug may be oily, or the points set too close. Possibly the spark is excessively advanced or the contact-breaker needs attention. Examine the h.t. cables for signs of shorting.

Fuel Consumption Excessive. If in spite of careful checking on the tuning of the carburettor, high fuel consumption continues, it is likely that one or more of the under-mentioned causes is responsible for wastage of precious fuel. Late ignition timing will eat into your petrol supplies quickly. The same applies to poor engine compression due to badly-fitting piston rings or valves. Also take into consideration the question of flooding due to a faulty float, air leakage at the joint between the carburettor and engine, weak valve springs. See that no wastage is caused by slack petrol-pipe union nuts.

AMAL CARBURETTOR MAINTENANCE

To ensure correct carburation it is advisable occasionally to remove the carburettor from the engine, strip it down completely, and then thoroughly clean it. It is a good plan to do this about every six months as described below.

Dismantling Standard Carburettor. First close both petrol taps and disconnect the twin petrol pipes from the carburettor by undoing the single union nut at the base of the float chamber. Referring to Fig. 3, loosen the jet plug (Q) and slacken the mixing chamber union nut (E).

Unscrew the mixing-chamber knurled cap-ring (Z) held by the retaining spring ($Z1$) at the top of the carburettor, and also remove the two nuts securing the carburettor flange to the face of the inlet port. Now remove the body of the carburettor, complete with the float chamber, from the engine.

When removing the carburettor, pull the air valve (D) and the throttle valve (B), together with the jet needle (C), from the body of the carburettor; temporarily tie up the slides out of the way. It is not necessary to remove the air and throttle slides from the control cables unless it is desired to renew the slides or control cables. The jet needle (C) can be adjusted for position in, or removed from, the throttle slide by removing the spring clip from the top of the slide. Examine the carburettor flange washer and, if damaged, renew it.

With the carburettor removed from the engine, proceed to remove the jet plug (Q) and the float chamber (R). Also remove the main jet (P) and the needle jet (O). Then completely unscrew the mixing-chamber union nut (E) and push the jet block (F) right out; if stiff, tap the jet block out gently with a wooden stump. Unscrew the float-chamber cover (*W*) after loosening the locking screw (*X*). Then withdraw the float by pinching the clip (*V*) inwards, and pull gently upwards.

Dismantling "Monobloc" Carburettor. Close both petrol taps and disconnect the twin petrol pipes by undoing the banjo bolt (8) over the

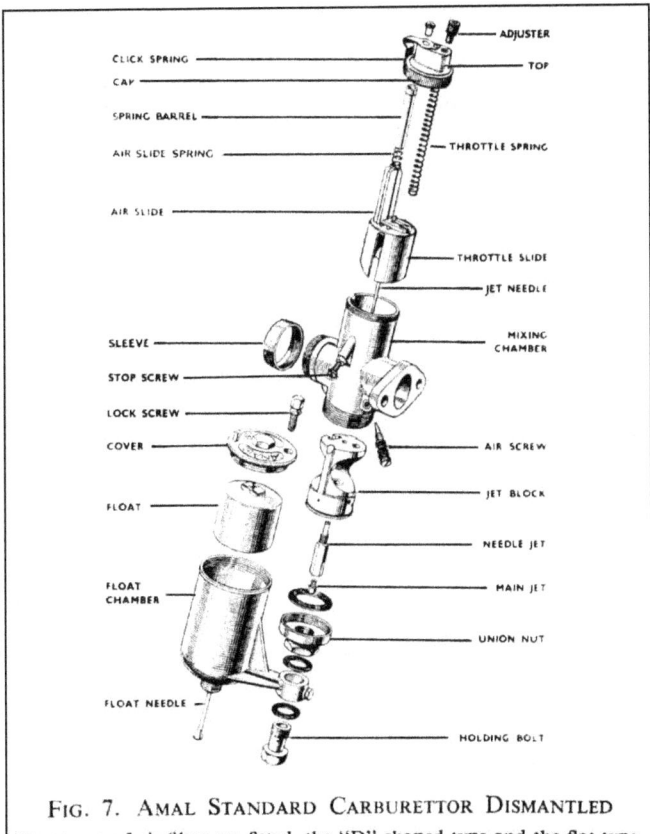

FIG. 7. AMAL STANDARD CARBURETTOR DISMANTLED
Two types of air filter are fitted, the "D"-shaped type and the flat type.

float chamber (*see* Fig. 5). Referring to Fig. 5, unscrew the mixing-chamber knurled cap-ring (2) on top of the carburettor and also remove the two nuts securing the carburettor flange to the face of the inlet port. Then remove the body of the carburettor (21), complete with the integral float chamber (13). While removing the carburettor, pull the air valve (3) and the throttle valve (24) from the mixing chamber and tie them up temporarily out of the way. As mentioned in the instructions for the standard type carburettor, it is rarely necessary to disconnect the slides from the cables. Check that the flange washer is sound.

Further dismantling is straightforward. Referring to Fig. 5, to remove the jet needle (23), withdraw the jet-needle clip (4) on top of the throttle valve, and remove the needle. To obtain access to the float (10), remove the three screws (11) securing the float-chamber cover (12). Lift out the hinged float (10) and withdraw the moulded-nylon needle (9). Lay both aside for cleaning. The float-chamber vent, by the way, is embodied in the tickler assembly (7), and the top-feed union houses a filter element of fine gauze which is readily accessible for cleaning.

To remove the main jet (14), remove the main-jet cover and unscrew the jet from the jet holder (15), which should also be unscrewed. Remove the jet-block locating screw (19) to the left of and slightly below the pilot air-adjusting screw. Then push or tap out the jet block (5) and fibre seal (22) through the large end of the mixing chamber (21). To remove the pilot jet (17), remove the pilot-jet cover nut and unscrew the jet.

Cleaning the Instrument. Wash all the carburettor components thoroughly clean with petrol and blow through the various ducts and passages to make sure that they are quite clear. Avoid using a fluffy rag for drying purposes. Pay special attention to the small pilot-jet passages in the jet block on both the standard and "Monobloc" type instruments. See that all impurities are removed from inside the float chamber. On the "Monobloc" carburettor do not forget to clean the detachable pilot jet and the filter gauze inside the top-feed union for the float chamber.

Inspecting the Parts. When dismantling the carburettor it is advisable to make a close inspection of the various parts if the carburettor has been in continuous service for a considerable period.

(1) *The Float Chamber.* Examine the components very carefully and check that the vent is unobstructed. The float must be in perfect condition. Clean the moulded-nylon needle on the "Monobloc" carburettor very thoroughly, and be careful not to damage it. On a standard carburettor hand-polish the valve part of the float needle by rotating the needle on its seat while pulling it vertically upwards. If a distinct shoulder is visible on the needle where it seats, renew the needle at once. Check for any sign of bending or distortion of the clip.

(2) *The Throttle Valve.* Test this for fit in the mixing chamber. Should excessive play exist, renew the slide forthwith. See that the new slide has the correct amount of cut-away.

(3) *The Jet-needle Clip.* The spring clip securing the tapered needle to the throttle valve must grip the needle firmly, and free rotation must *not* occur, as this causes the needle groove to wear. Always be careful to replace the needle with the clip in the correct groove.

(4) *The Jet Block.* Before tapping this home in the mixing chamber

verify by blowing that the pilot-jet ducts are clear and that the jet-block fibre seal is in good condition.

(5) *The Carburettor Flange.* Examine this for truth with a straight-edge. Distortion sometimes occurs, and this may cause an air leak. If the flange face is slightly concave, file and rub down the face with emery cloth laid on a surface plate until it is dead flat and smooth. Alternatively have it faced on a machine.

Assembling Standard Carburettor. Referring to Fig. 3, refit the jet block (F) with the fibre washer on its under side, and screw on lightly the mixing-chamber union nut (E). Screw in the needle jet (O) and the main jet (P). Open the air lever $\frac{7}{8}$ in. and the throttle twist-grip half-way; grasp the air slide between the thumb and the finger and make sure that the jet needle enters the central hole in the barrel (H). Slightly turn the throttle slide until it enters the barrel guide when, on pushing down the slides, the air valve should enter its guide. If not, slightly move the mixing-chamber cap (Y), when the air valve will slide into position. Screw home the mixing-chamber knurled cap-ring (Z). No force is necessary.

Replace the carburettor-flange washer, offer up the carburettor body, and secure in position by tightening evenly the two nuts. Replace the float and needle in the float chamber, holding the needle against its seating with a pencil until the float (T) and needle clip (V) are slipped into position. See that the spring clip enters the needle groove. Then screw home the float-chamber cover securely and lock in position by tightening the lock-screw (X).

Insert the jet plug (Q) in the union nut (E) and very firmly tighten the union nut with a suitable spanner. Remove the jet plug and fit the float chamber and secure with the jet plug. Be sure there is a fibre washer above and below the float-chamber lug as shown in Fig. 7. When the float chamber has been correctly positioned, tighten the jet plug firmly. Finally reconnect the twin petrol pipes and tighten the union nut at the base of the float chamber. In the event of the pilot-jet adjustment having been disturbed, re-tune as described on page 16.

Wear of Jet Needle. The needle itself does *not* wear, though some wear of the groove may occur if the jet-needle clip is not grasping the needle firmly. If the mixture is too rich with the clip in No. 1 groove (nearest top end), it is probable that the needle jet needs to be renewed because of wear. It is assumed that the carburettor is correctly tuned and that no flooding occurs.

Assembling "Monobloc" Carburettor. Do this in the reverse order of dismantling. Referring to Fig. 5, screw home the pilot jet (17) and the pilot-jet cover nut, not omitting to replace its washer. Push or tap home the jet block (5) and fibre seal (22) through the large end of the mixing chamber (21). Check that the fibre seal fitted to the stub of the jet block is in good condition. Then fit the jet block locating-screw (19). Screw the main-jet holder (15) into the jet block, after checking that the washer for the holder is sound. Next screw the main jet (16) into the jet holder.

Replace the moulded-nylon needle (9) in the float chamber (13), and fit the hinged float (10) with the *narrow* side of the hinge uppermost. Afterwards fit the float-chamber cover (12) and secure by means of the three screws (11). Verify that the cover and body faces are undamaged and quite clean. Renew the washer.

If previously removed, attach the jet needle (23) to the throttle valve (24) and secure with the jet-needle clip (4), making sure that the clip enters the correct groove.

Position the carburettor-flange washer, and offer up the carburettor to the face of the inlet port after easing the air and throttle valves (3) and (24) down into the mixing chamber (*see* hints on page 21 concerning the standard carburettor). When easing the throttle valve home, make sure that the tapered jet needle (23) really enters the hole in the jet block (5). Secure the carburettor flange firmly to the engine by means of the two nuts, and tighten these evenly. Tighten down firmly the mixing-chamber knurled cap-ring (2) and see that the throttle slide works freely when this is tightened down.

Finally reconnect the twin petrol pipes by tightening the banjo bolt (8) over the float chamber (13).

Concerning Joint Gaskets. On 1945–59 models 5T and T100 it is advisable to coat the joint gaskets between the induction manifold and the cylinder head with suitable jointing compound. By doing this the thin paper washers are prevented from weaving between two dissimilar metals and thereby partially obstructing the induction apertures.

THE AIR FILTER

Dismantling the Filter. *Rigid-frame Models.* To remove the filter for servicing, the battery and battery carrier must first be removed. Disconnect the rubber sleeve and remove the filter.

Swinging arm-frame Models. On all except models 3TA and 5TA the oil tank must first be detached by the removal of the three fixing bolts and disconnexion of the oil pipes. Disconnect the rubber sleeve and remove the filter.

On the earlier type models 3TA and 5TA to remove the filter it is necessary to remove the rear panels from the machine. On later models of the same type, remove the battery and battery carrier. Then remove the air-filter top bolt and lift the filter clear of the bottom spigot.

Servicing. Unscrew the two screws securing the cover, remove the cover and extract the element of the "D"-shaped filter (*see* Fig. 8). In the case of the flat-type filter, remove the cover to which the element is attached (*see* Fig. 9).

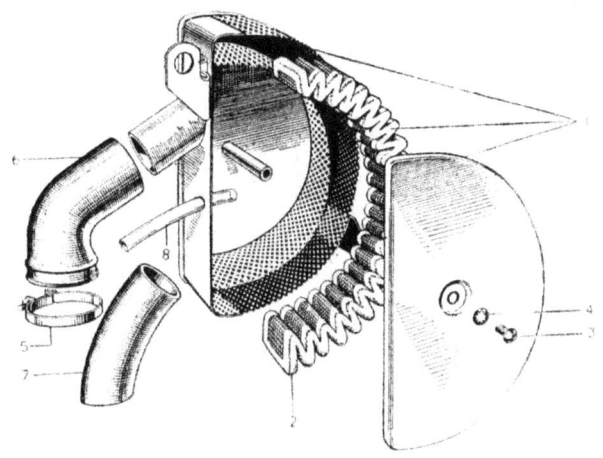

FIG. 8 "D"-SHAPED TYPE AIR FILTER

1. Filter assembly
2. Filter element
3. Cover screw
4. Shakeproof washer
5. Clip connexion to carburettor
6. Connexion, Amal carburettor to filter (rubber)
7. Connexion, S.U. carburettor to filter (rubber)
8. Vent pipe, carburettor to filter

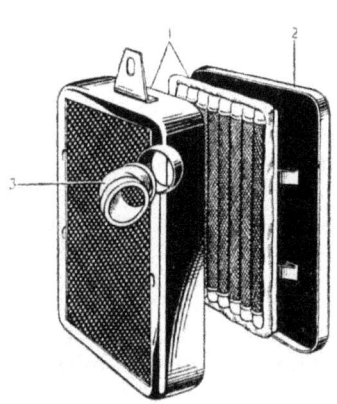

FIG. 9. FLAT TYPE AIR FILTER

1. Filter assembly
2. Element with cover
3. Connexion sleeve (rubber)

Remove the filter element and wash it in petrol or paraffin until all dust is extracted after every 2,000 miles running, then dry off the element thoroughly. When dry, re-oil with "Vokes Trifiltrene" filter oil or SAE 20 grade oil.

Change the filter element after every 10,000 miles. A choked filter causes loss of performance and heavy fuel consumption.

The maximum power output is little affected with the air filter attached.

THE S.U. M.C.2 CARBURETTOR

The S.U. carburettor is of the automatically expanding type in which the cross sectional area of the air passage and the effective orifice of the jet is variable.

Adjustment and Tuning. It is not advisable that the needle type which governs the effective orifice of the jet should be changed from the maker's original specification, as this is determined for a particular engine after considerable testing, both on the engine test bed and on road test with premium grade petrols. Low grade and alcohol-blended fuels may require the fitting of a richer than standard needle.

If in doubt regarding the correctness of the type fitted, check by removing the suction chamber, then by slackening the side needle screw when the needle can be removed and its markings by numbers or letters noted. These identifying markings may be rolled round the shank, or stamped on the flat end. Only this needle should be changed to alter the mixture strength, as all jets are of standard size and the jet adjusting nut is for setting the idling only. It is essential that the needle be fitted with its shoulder flush with the face of the piston, as shown in Fig. 10.

When detaching the suction chamber and piston assembly from the main carburettor body to check or change the needle, remove the oil cap and the two side screws and lift the assembly off the carburettor body.

Tuning the carburettor is confined to correct idling adjustment by means of the throttle-stop screw, which governs the amount of throttle opening for idling speed, and the jet adjusting nut (Fig. 10) which controls the idling mixture. Screwing this nut up weakens the mixture, screwing it down enriches it. This nut must not be forced, as this may set the jet off centre.

A too rich idling mixture gives a rhythmical or regular misfire with a trace of black in the exhaust. A too weak mixture gives an irregular type of misfire with a tendency to stop. A correct mixture gives an even beat with a colourless exhaust.

Defects in Operation. Faults other than carburation may be causes of erratic engine running, so consider first the following—

(a) Compression: Check for equal pressure in both cylinders; check tappets.

CORRECT CARBURATION

(b) Moisture Condensation: Examine float chamber and H.T. cables.
(c) Ignition: Inspect distributor points, clean and adjust if necessary. Contact-breaker and condenser condition is most important. Sparking plugs should be cleaned and re-gapped. Correct timing is essential for good idling; particularly excessive advance and faulty operation of the automatic mechanism must be corrected.
(d) Check for Air Leaks: Between the manifold and cylinder head; between the manifold and carburettor; between the two halves of the carburettor; and at the suction chamber cap.

If no faults are found in the engine and ignition, check the following points on the carburettor.

PISTON STICKING. This fault is easily detected. The symptoms are stalling and refusal of the engine to run slowly, or lack of power with excessive petrol consumption. The piston should rest on the bridge when the engine is not running. It should drop freely and hit the bridge sharply and distinctly when raised by hand through the air intake; to check, the filter rubber connexion must be removed.

The cause may be dirt or contact between the piston and suction chamber, or sticking of the piston rod in its bush.

If the suction chamber, piston or piston rod are dirty or corroded, clean with a solvent—petrol, thinners, degreasing fluid or alcohol—but no abrasive should be used. Reassemble when clean and dry and apply oil to the piston rod only.

If there is metallic contact, remove the high spot by very careful use of a scraper—careless scraping will render the parts scrap.

LUBRICATION. Remove the plastic oil-cap from the top of the suction chamber every month, or as often as may be necessary, and oil the piston rod and guide bush assembly thoroughly with thin machine-oil. See that the cap is firmly screwed down after replacing the oil cap and washer—an air leak upsets the automatic operation of the piston in the suction chamber, causing a rich setting and loss of speed.

FLOODING FROM FLOAT CHAMBER OR JET. The cause may be a punctured float or dirt between the float-chamber needle-valve and its seating. To correct either fault, remove the float chamber lid and clean, replace the float or effect any repair necessary.

Flooding may also occur if the manufacturer's original setting of the float-needle hinged lever (Fig. 10) in the top of the float chamber has been disturbed. The setting figure for the fork is that with the fork pressing the needle home on its seating; a $\frac{3}{8}$-in. (9·5-mm) diameter test bar should just slide between the curve of the fork and the circular facing of the float-lid casing.

A bad seal between the float needle and its seating may also cause flooding. This can sometimes be restored by tapping the needle lightly with a delicate instrument, such as the handle of a screwdriver.

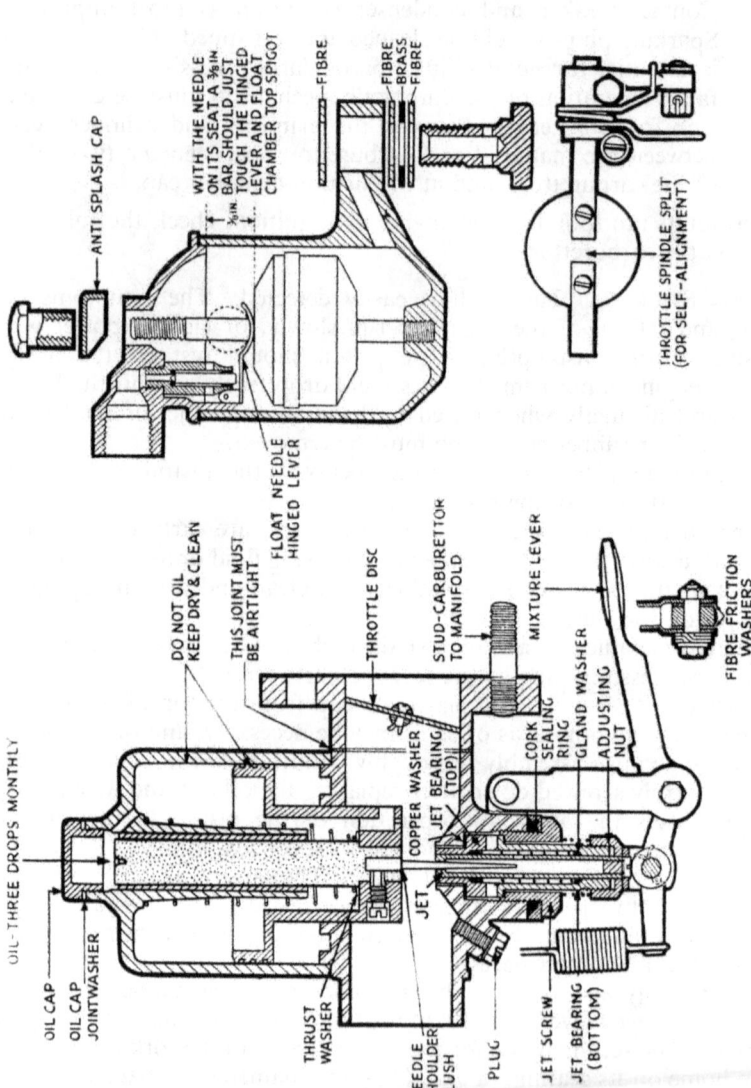

FIG. 10. SECTIONED ARRANGEMENT OF S.U. M.C.2 CARBURETTOR

If slow leaking near the jet head is noticed, it is likely that the jet-gland washer and its lower counterpart, together with the cork sealing ring require replacement. The mixture lever should be detached from the jet head, the jet screw removed, and the entire jet and jet-bush assembly withdrawn. Take great care when assembling to replace all parts in their correct positions as shown in Fig. 10.

AIR FILTER. The rider is warned not to disconnect the air filter with the idea of increasing the maximum speed. The carburettor and air filter together give maximum efficiency; the removal of the filter impairs the general performance of the machine, as the carburettor is exposed to road dust and other foreign matter. The free movement of the piston in the suction chamber is vital to the satisfactory operation of the carburettor, of the engine and, therefore, of the whole machine; the freedom of the piston is restricted if the air filter is removed.

PETROL TAP ADJUSTMENT

When adjusting, replacing or repairing the petrol tap, the fuel must be drained from the tank.

PUSH-PULL TYPE. The adjustment of a leaking tap is made by first removing the grub screw locking the plunger to the body, then the plunger assembly can be removed. Grip the plunger end in a suitable tool and turn the knob in a clockwise direction; this expands the cork washer and makes a petrol-tight fit when the washer is replaced in the petrol tap body. A new cork should be fitted if the original one has deteriorated to any extent.

TAPER TYPE. Remove the faulty tap and dismantle; take out the split-pin, remove the washer, spring back-plate and withdraw the spindle and then apply a light smear of fine grinding-in paste to the spindle; add a little oil and rotate the spindle in the tap body using the same movement as when grinding-in the valves. When a good surface is obtained, wash the parts in petrol, dry and apply tallow fat to the spindle before assembly. Check the tension of the spring and, if not enough, stretch it a little.

CHAPTER III

TRIUMPH LUBRICATION

THE oil film between the several contacting surfaces of the working parts of a motor-cycle is equal in importance to the quality of the materials used in making the various components of the machine. Adequate and proper lubrication means supplying a sufficient quantity of the right kind of oil or grease. If the quantity of lubricant is sufficient but the quality is low and the grade incorrect or, on the other hand, if the quality and grade are correct but the supply deficient, trouble is certain to be encountered and the serviceable life of the motor-cycle reduced.

ENGINE LUBRICATION SYSTEM

The engine operates at a high speed and this is conducive to comparatively high temperatures, so it is imperative that only oils of the best and proved quality be used. Lubricant in constant circulation collects many substances, such as unburnt fuel, moisture through condensation, carbon, and gritty and metallic particles of an abrasive nature; these all create wear and should be extracted without delay. The selection of the oil is in the hands of the motor-cyclist, and it is also his duty to look after the system. Recommended lubricants are listed on page 41.

Dry Sump System (1937–9 Models). All 1937–9 models are fitted with dry-sump lubrication.

The engine oil is fed from the oil tank beneath the saddle through a pipe to the pressure side of the oil pump (*see* Fig. 12). The pump then forces the oil through the drilled crankshaft assembly to the big-end(s) where it emerges in the form of mist which thoroughly lubricates the internal components of the power unit.

On the 1939 twin-cylinder Triumph engines, the oil pressure is regulated by means of a release valve situated in the centre of the timing case. The release valve comprises a ball which is normally held on its seat by means of a coil spring. When, however, the pressure of the oil rises above normal, the ball is raised off its seat and permits surplus oil to flow to the bottom of the crankcase. Thus the pressure of the release-valve spring automatically determines the oil pressure, assuming that the oil is circulating properly. Oil after circulating through the engine falls to the bottom of the crankcase through a large gauze filter, and is then picked up by the suction side of the oil pump and forced back into the oil tank. It should be noted that on the 1938 twin-cylinder engine ("Speed Twin") there is no ball release-valve in the centre of the timing case. There is, however, a piston-type valve situated in the timing cover. This feeds oil into the crankshaft and by-passes a certain quantity into the timing case. Owing

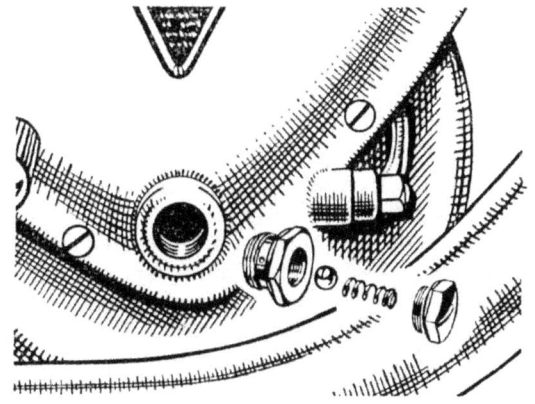

Fig. 11. Oil-pressure Release Valve (1939 Twins)

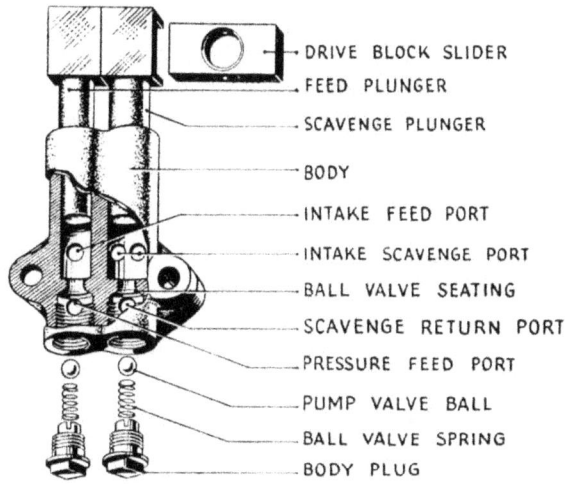

Fig. 12. Oil Pump (1937–59)

to the design of this valve, trouble due to oil impurities is never likely to occur.

The capacity of the suction side of the pump is twice as great as that of the delivery or pressure side, and this ensures that the engine sump remains "dry." The delivery pipe on the O.H.V. models is tapped, a by-pass pipe (external) leading some of the oil direct to the rocker box. Oil from the rocker box on twin-cylinder engines is conveyed by pipes to the upper ends of the push-rod tubes and is returned by gravity to the crankcase after lubricating the cams and tappet gear.

Dry Sump System (1945–59 Models). The dry-sump lubrication system is employed on all 1945–59 Triumph models. The oil is gravity-fed from the oil tank through a filter and pipe to the pressure side of the oil pump. The pump (*see* Fig. 12) is a double-plunger type, fitted with two non-return valves. The oil is forced through drilled passage-ways to the crankshaft, and from the big-ends the oil issues as a fog to lubricate the pistons and other internal engine parts.

A release valve in the timing cover (*see* Fig. 13) controls the oil pressure. This valve serves two purposes; to release excessive oil-pressure and to indicate the pressure by visible means. It consists of a piston, main spring, secondary spring, oil seal and button indicator. The valve is forced back on the secondary spring when the engine is running, this being shown by the button protruding through the cover nut. The piston is moved still farther back on the main spring when the oil pressure is excessive, thus allowing oil to be by-passed through the release-valve body to the crankcase where it is scavenged to the oil tank.

After passing through the engine, oil falls to the bottom of the crankcase where it is filtered. The crankcase oil return pipe (visible as it protrudes through the filter when the sump plate is removed) then returns the oil to the suction side of the oil pump to be returned to the oil tank. The suction oil-pump plunger has double the capacity of the pressure side; this ensures that no liquid oil remains on the floor of the crankcase. The valve rockers are lubricated by oil taken from the return scavenge pipe by tapping the supply just below the oil tank. After being forced through the rocker spindles, the oil lubricates the valve stems and push-rod cups. External drain pipes are fitted on all models; these pipes collect the oil from the valve wells in the cylinder head and transfer it to the push-rod cover tubes, where it lubricates the tappets and finally drains into the sump.

LUBRICATING ENGINE

Engine (1937–9 Models). About every 250 miles remove the filler cap of the oil tank, inspect the oil level and, if necessary, top up with suitable engine oil (*see* page 41). The tank should preferably be kept filled to within 2 in. of the filler orifice, that is just below the opening of the return pipe. On no account must the level of oil be allowed to fall below the minimum level mark. When changing the oil the tank should be flushed out with flushing oil (obtainable from most garages and accessory dealers). It is not necessary to discard the flushing oil after use as this may be filtered through a piece of muslin and used again. It is also important when changing the oil to remove and clean the filters. Two filters are provided, one in the oil tank and one in the crankcase. On 1939 twin-cylinder models there is an additional filter incorporated in the oil pressure release-valve body on the timing case.

To remove the tank filter disconnect the two feed pipes by withdrawing them from their rubber connecting tubes. Then unscrew the large hexagonal nut on the tank and remove this together with the filter. To remove the crankcase filter undo the four hexagonal-headed screws which secure the filter to the crankcase and remove the baseplate and filter. Removal of the filter in the pressure release valve on the 1939 twin-cylinder models is merely a question of unscrewing the body from the timing case (*see* Fig. 11). Having removed the filters wash them thoroughly in petrol and avoid using a fluffy rag on the gauze. When replacing the crankcase filter, see that the washers are undamaged and clean and tighten the screws evenly. As soon as the engine starts, check the oil pressure at the gauge on the instrument panel and also remove the tank filter cap and note if the oil is being returned.

With the Triumph design of oil pump all parts are constantly immersed in oil, and wear, therefore, takes place very slowly. Hence do not immediately suspect the pump when some lubrication trouble arises. It is very unlikely to be responsible. The only part likely to wear after a very considerable mileage is the pump drive block which may be replaced for a small sum.

A possible cause of the Triumph pump not working satisfactorily is imperfect seating of the two spring-loaded ball valves at the foot of the pump (*see* Fig. 12). To rectify the trouble, remove the balls and clean them and their seats thoroughly. In extreme instances it may be desirable to remove the pump body from the engine, and sharply tap the balls on to their seats before reassembling. When replacing the oil pump cover, see that the joint washer is absolutely clean and intact; also be sure to re-tighten the cover screws evenly and firmly.

Engine (1945–59). The lubrication system of the 1945–59 Triumph models is so simple that it functions for a long time without attention to the actual pumping mechanism. It will readily be realized, however, that the duties of changing the oil and cleaning the filters must be carried out at regular intervals (*see* pages 38 and 40). Failure to observe this elementary precaution may cause a complete breakdown due to foreign matter entering the system.

The scavenge side of the oil pump has double the capacity of the feed side, so if the oil-tank cap is removed (after the engine has been started) it will be seen that the return of oil to the tank via the stack pipe (visible just inside the filter aperture) is spasmodic. This arrangement keeps the crankcase sump free of oil, under normal running conditions, as the scavenger pump draws air until the crankcase scavenge pipe is again submerged in oil. The air which is forced into the oil tank is vented out through an outlet pipe into the primary chaincase.

If a lubrication fault should eventuate, the following may help you to find the trouble—

Oil Tank. Check to determine whether the amount of oil in the tank is correct—it should be within 1½ in. (4 cm) of the filler cap and no more. Suitable engine oils are given on page 41. *See also* page 43. On models

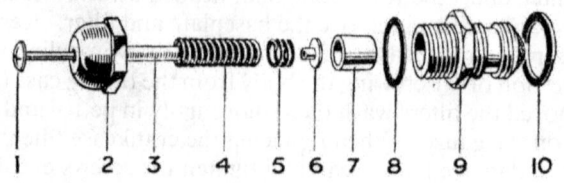

FIG. 13. OIL-PRESSURE RELEASE VALVE AND INDICATOR (1945–59)

1. Indicator shaft and button
2. Valve cap
3. Rubber seal
4. Main spring
5. Auxiliary spring
6. Shaft nut
7. Piston
8. Cap washer
9. Body
10. Body washer

3TA and 5TA raise the twinseat (*see* Fig. 60) to get at the tank. See that the vent pipe is clear; any obstruction will cause a back-pressure in the oil tank, which will prevent adequate scavenging by the oil pump with the result that the crankcase is flooded.

Oil Pump. The oil-pump block is the only part likely to show wear, and this only after a considerable mileage; it can be replaced very cheaply. The wear of the plungers and pump body (*see* Fig. 12) is negligible as they are constantly immersed in oil. These parts can, therefore, be ignored if the lubrication is at fault.

The pump will not function correctly, if the non-return valve balls are not seating properly. In this case, remove the oil pump and unscrew the two plugs located under the oil pump body to allow the balls and springs to be removed (*see* Fig. 12). Wash all parts in petrol to remove any dirt; when replacing the balls give them a sharp tap on to their seatings before reassembly. Before fitting, prime the pump with oil.

Oil Release Valve and Indicator. No maintenance is required other than cleaning, as this unit is very reliable. When the oil is changed, however, it is advisable to dismantle the unit and wash it thoroughly in petrol so that the piston will work freely in the release-valve body (*see* Fig. 13). In no circumstances tamper with the release-valve springs, as the spring poundage is set to give correct oil pressure. Only genuine Triumph spares should be bought to replace these springs, if the occasion arises when replacement is necessary.

Oil Pipes (*Tank to Engine*). Care must be exercised when replacing the rubber connexions of the oil pipes so that chafing the inside is prevented. If chafing occurs, it is possible that a small piece of rubber may enter the oil system and this, on reaching the oil pump, would cause lack of pressure to the crankshaft. Any foreign matter in the scavenge pipe-line above the pump is returned to the oil tank (the rocker oil feed may be blocked in exceptional cases) and is prevented from entering the oil system by the tank filter.

Crankcase Scavenge Pipe. The oil will not scavenge from the crankcase if the pipe is cracked or there is an air leak between the pipe and the crankcase, but this is very unlikely to happen. The trouble would only become apparent when the engine is hot. A simple test, if this be suspected is to remove the crankcase sump plate and filter and to fix a length of rubber tubing over the scavenge pipe. If the open end of the rubber tube be placed in the mouth and sucked, the tubing will collapse if the scavenge pipe is air-tight; it will not collapse if there is a leak. If this be the fault, the engine must be removed and stripped before it can be rectified.

Valve Rockers, Rocker Spindles and Push-rods. The oil feed to the rocker spindles is supplied by the scavenge side of the main oil-supply. The only thing which can cause a lack of oil to the rockers is a stoppage in the oil pipe-line. This can be rectified by removing the pipe and checking by forcing air through it. To check the oil supply at the spindle, run the engine until it is warm so that the oil temperature is increased and then slacken off the two acorn nuts, which secure the oil pipe banjos to the rocker spindles, when a regular drip of oil should continue. If the motorcycle has been "laid-up" for some time, it is advantageous to flood the rocker mechanism. To flood this mechanism, start the engine and then remove the oil tank filler cap, and a finger should be placed over the scavenge outlet pipe so that the oil is forced through the rocker spindles, rockers and to the push-rods.

Changing the Oil. *See* page 38.

Recommended Engine Oils. *See* page 41.

Cleaning the Filters. *See* page 40.

Magneto Lubrication. *See* page 46.

The Distributor Units (Coil Ignition). *See* pages 52, 58.

THE MOTOR-CYCLE PARTS

Gearbox. After every 1,000 miles running, the oil level should be brought up to that of the level plug.

In the case of a brand-new machine it is advisable to drain and refill the gearbox after the first 500 miles and subsequently at intervals of 5,000 miles.

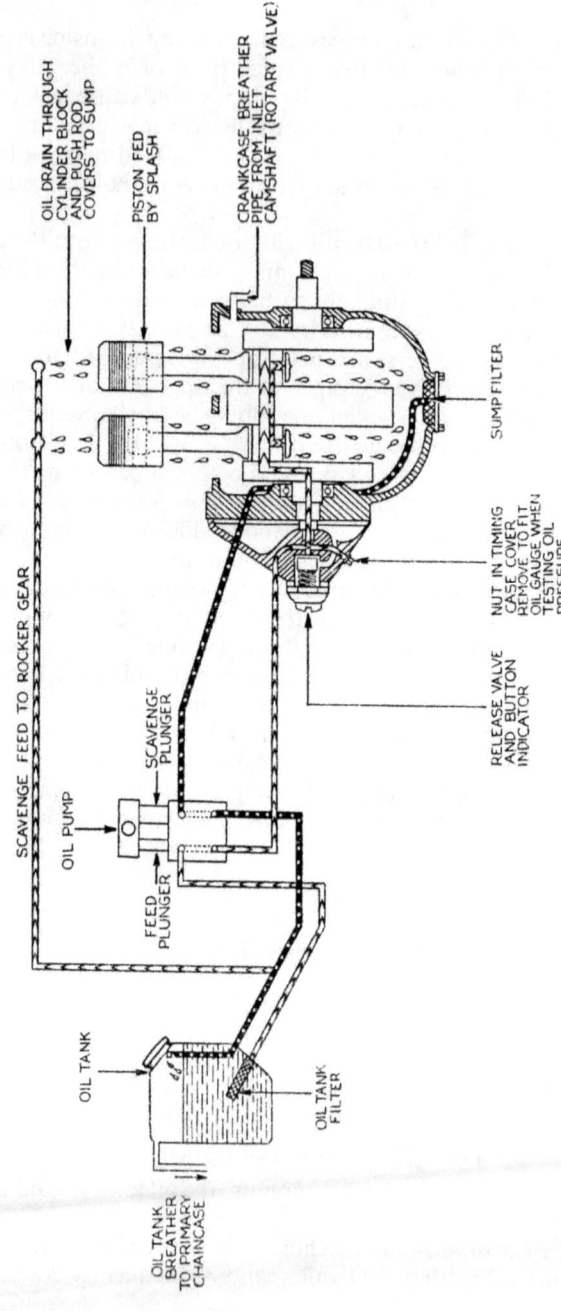

Fig. 14. Diagram of Lubrication System (All Models Except 3TA and 5TA)

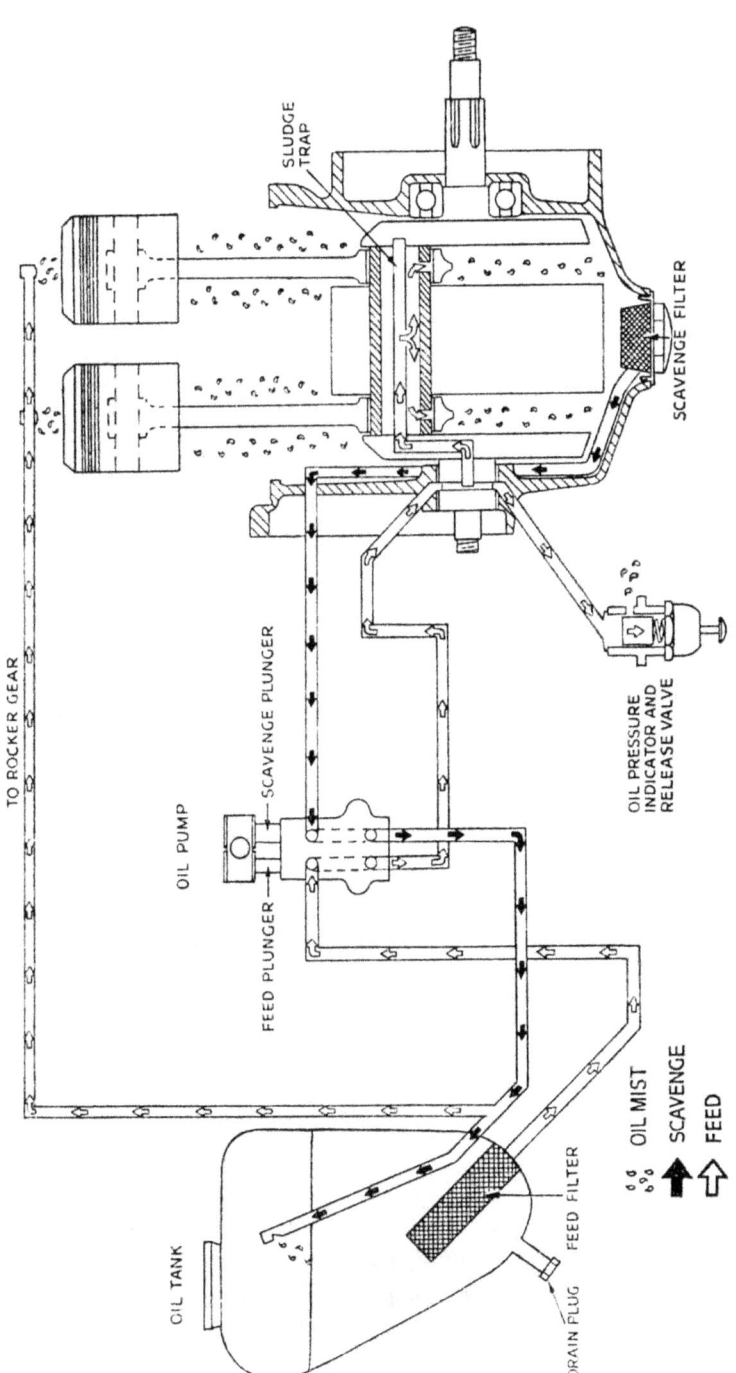

Fig. 15. Diagram of Lubrication System (Models 3TA and 5TA)

On 1937–9 models the level plug is situated at the back of the kick-starter casing underneath the tool box. Care should be taken never to over-fill the gearbox and in no circumstances should thick gear-oil be used for replenishment. Before topping-up the gearbox always make sure that the level plug is first removed, otherwise excessive lubricant will enter the box and cause leakage and heavy gear-changing. About every 5,000 miles the drain plug should be removed and the gearbox completely drained, flushed out and replenished with fresh oil. The drain plug will be found at the back of the gearbox.

The gearbox of the 1945–59 Triumphs is lubricated by (*see* page 41) oil and in no circumstances should a heavy viscous oil or grease be used. Splash oil is fed to all parts, including the enclosed footchange and kick-starter mechanism, so that complete lubrication is ensured.

Primary Chaincase (1937–9 Models). On those models on which primary drive oil-bath cases are fitted, inspect occasionally and keep the oil up to the level plug; this part should be drained every 1,000 miles, using the base plug. The vent in the filler plug must be kept clear.

Models having chain covers have a positive oil feed to the primary chain, and the flow is readily adjustable as this supply is taken from the main engine oil line; the pressure requires only a slight opening on the regulator. The nozzle of the pipe should be properly directed adjacent to the chain links. Rear chain lubrication is automatic on all models, by crankcase ventilation breathing through a pipe to a point near the gearbox sprocket on early models. On these models it is important to keep the release clear. It is unlikely that trouble will be experienced, but should the secondary chain be noticed running dry, it will be necessary to detach the primary oil-bath chaincase and remove and clean the oil pipe and disc valve on the crankcase. Do this with petrol. No adjustment of the release valve is ever needed.

On 1939 models the secondary chain is lubricated by an adjustable lubricator situated at the rear of the primary chaincase. Lubricating oil from the chaincase is fed by splash into a small receptacle, and from here it is supplied to the secondary chain in an amount determined by the adjustment of the regulator screw. The screw should be adjusted so that the chain receives just sufficient lubrication. To commence with, unscrew the regulator $2\frac{1}{2}$ turns from the fully-home position. About every 1,000 miles in summer and every 1,500 miles in winter the secondary chain should be removed, immersed in a bath of paraffin and dried. It should then be submerged in a bath of graphite grease and oil heated over a tin of boiling water. See that the grease penetrates into all the chain bearings before refitting the chain. When refitting on the sprockets, make sure that the spring link has the open end facing *away from* the direction of motion.

Primary Chaincase (1945–59 Models). The primary chaincase houses the clutch, primary-drive chain, engine sprocket and, in the case of models

5T, 6T, 3TA and 5TA, also the alternator unit. Care should be taken to maintain the correct oil-level; if the correct grade of oil (*see* page 41) is employed, the lubricant qualities are not reduced by condensation. A burnt-out clutch, chain failure and perhaps damage to the alternator unit (where fitted) may result if the rider fails to follow these simple instructions. If a too-high viscosity oil (above SAE 20) is used, that is, above oils as listed on page 41, the clutch plates will be difficult to separate thus causing noisy gear-changing.

Grease Nipples. All components provided with grease nipples for lubricating purposes should be attended to at regular intervals. The

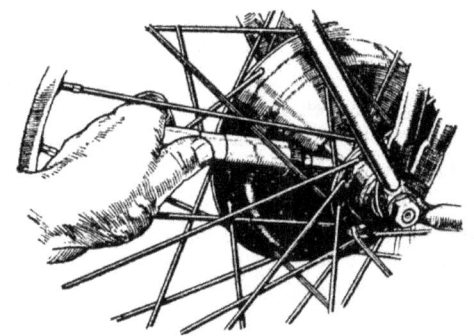

FIG. 16. APPLICATION OF GREASE GUN (1937–9 HUB)

lubricants recommended for use in the grease gun are given on page 41. If a heavier grade is used, the various bearings and bushes may be starved, with consequent rapid wear. The manner in which the grease gun is used is shown in Fig. 16.

All important motor-cycle components on the 1945–59 series of Triumph models, such as brakes and swinging-fork mechanism, are provided with grease nipples. Only the recommended grades (*see* page 41) should be used; neither heavier nor lighter grades will ensure proper lubrication. Note that no provision is made for greasing the steering head and wheel bearings; the bearings on assembly are packed with grease and no further greasing is necessary until they are examined for general wear and tear.

Chains. The primary (front) chain is enclosed and positively lubricated (*see* page 40). The secondary chain is lubricated by controlled oil splash from the primary chaincase. An oil trough in the rear of the inner chaincase and a hole drilled to atmosphere is the method adopted. In the outer cover a corresponding hole is drilled and tapped, into which a tapered needle valve is screwed, the taper entering the hole in the inner cover. To decrease or increase the oil supply to the secondary chain, screw the valve in or out.

Note that on models 3TA and 5TA the metering jet in the feed pipe should not be cleaned with wire if it is obstructed; the correct procedure is to blow it out with compressed air.

Clutch Lubrication (1945-59 Models). The Triumph multi-plate clutch runs in oil and it is therefore imperative to keep the primary chaincase replenished with the correct type of oil to the correct level. The correct type of oil is stated on page 41. Failure to maintain proper chaincase lubrication is likely to cause the friction inserts of the clutch plates to burn and disintegrate under heavy loading.

The Steering Head. No grease nipples are provided. About every 10,000 miles repack the bearing races with suitable grease.

Wheel Hubs. These are well packed with grease for the bearings, and this would suffice for 10,000 and 20,000 miles in the case of rigid and spring wheels respectively.

Brake Lubrication. Oil occasionally all exposed joints and cables, and do not forget the rear brake pedal shaft. Every 1,000 miles apply the grease gun to the nipples for the brake cam spindles. Do not over-grease.

Controls. At intervals the control cables should be lubricated; stiffness in operation results if they become dry. A good plan is to remove the Bowden wire connexion from the lever at its top and make a funnel with brown paper round the casing, fastening it with a rubber band. If thin machine oil is fed into the funnel, and allowed to remain overnight, it will trickle down the casing and lubricate the cable. Keep the control cables clear of the engine; if they become over-heated the lubricant dries up.

The Triumph twist-grip throttle control is not likely to require any attention.

All brake rod joints and pins should be lubricated by means of the oil-can.

CHANGING THE OIL

During the running-in period the oil in the oil tank and gearbox should be changed frequently when the machine is new, so that any foreign matter which may be picked up by the oil as it circulates is eliminated.

OIL TANK. The oil should be changed at 250, 500 and 1,000 miles during the running-in period and regularly every 1,500 miles thereafter. When changing the oil, the oil tank and crankcase filters must be cleaned thoroughly in petrol.

Before changing the oil it is advisable to flush out the oil tank with a proprietary flushing oil (obtainable from most accessory firms). In the event of the oil tank being found very dirty, remove it from the motorcycle and thoroughly clean it. Note that the oil tank should always be drained after a run when the oil is *warm*.

After draining the oil tank, cleaning the filters, and replenishing the tank with fresh oil, check with a spanner that all nuts previously removed

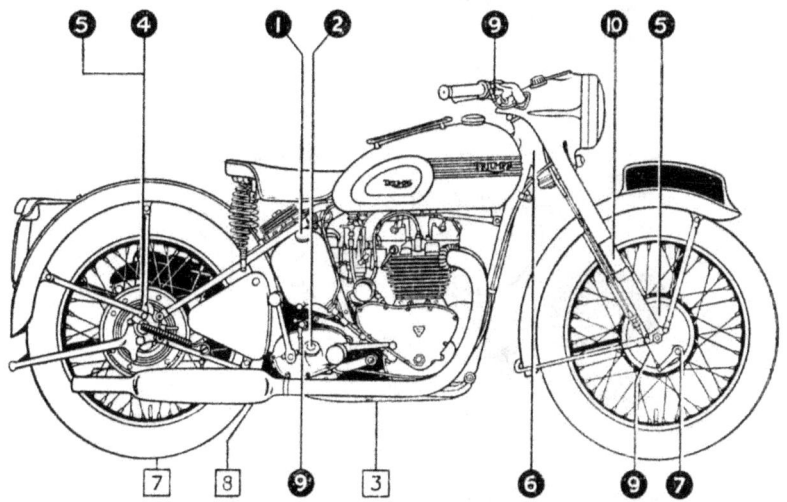

FIG. 17. LUBRICATION CHART (RIGID FRAME MODELS)

Numbers in circles refer to off-side of machine.

No.	Part	SAE	No.	Part	SAE
1.	Engine Oil Tank	20 or 30	7.	Brake Cam Spindle	Grease
2.	Gearbox	30	8.	Footbrake Pedal Spindle	Grease
3.	Primary Chaincase	20	9.	Exposed Cables	20
4.	Spring Wheel	Grease	10.	Fork (hydraulic)	20
5.	Wheel Hubs	Grease		OIL-CAN LUBRICATION All Brake-rod Joints and Pins	20
6.	Steering Head	Grease			

are firmly (not excessively) tightened and that there is no oil leakage from any of the joints. After starting up the engine, check immediately that the engine oil is being returned to the tank and that the oil indicator button (*see* Fig. 13) is projecting from the timing case cover. As has been mentioned on page 32, it is advantageous to dismantle and clean the oil-pressure release valve and indicator unit when periodically changing the engine oil every 1,500 miles.

OIL TANK FILTER. To remove, unscrew the union nut attaching the feed pipe to the tank and the large, hexagonal nut to which the filter is fitted. On earlier 3TA models it is necessary to remove the panels from the machine, but on all later models the filter is accessible from below.

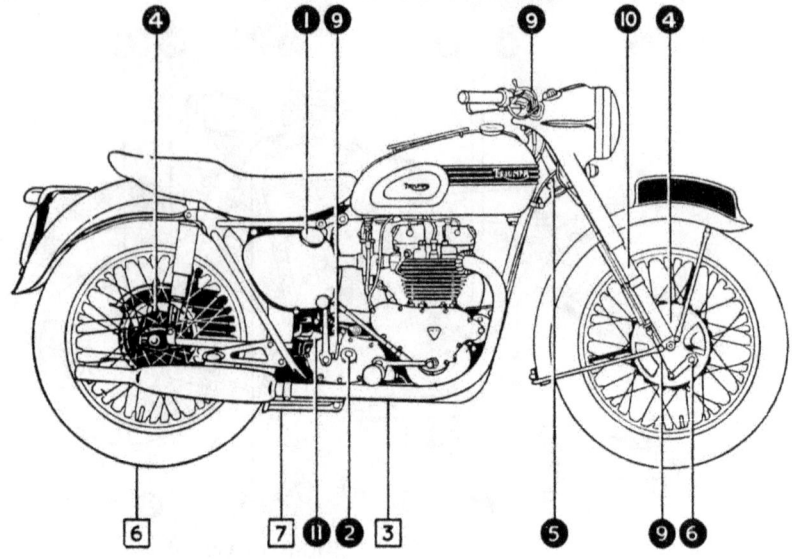

FIG. 18. LUBRICATION CHART ("SWINGING ARM" MODELS)

Numbers in circles refer to off-side of motor-cycle. For lubrication chart applicable to models 3TA, 5TA, see Fig. 19.

No.	PART	SAE	No.	PART	SAE
1.	Engine Oil Tank	20 or 30	7.	Footbrake Pedal Spindle	Grease
2.	Gearbox	30	9.	Exposed Cables	20
3.	Primary Chaincase	20	10.	Fork (hydraulic)	20
4.	Wheel Hubs	Grease	11.	Swinging-fork Spindle	Grease
5.	Steering Head	Grease		OIL-CAN LUBRICATION All Brake-rod Joints and Pins	20
6.	Brake Cam Spindle	Grease			

CRANKCASE FILTER. This filter is in the base of the crankcase. To remove it, unscrew the four hexagon-headed screws (on late models the sump plate is secured by four nuts). Carefully withdraw the filter to avoid damage to the gauze.

PRIMARY CHAINCASE. Change the oil in the primary chaincase every

RECOMMENDED LUBRICANTS (UNITED KINGDOM)

Unit	Esso	Wakefield	Shell	Mobil	B.P.
Engine Summer Winter	Essolube 30 Essolube 20	Castrol XL Castrolite	Shell X-100 30 Shell X-100 20/20 W	Mobiloil A Mobiloil Arctic	Energol SAE 30 Energol SAE 20
Gearbox	Essolube 30	Castrol GP	Shell X-100 50	Mobiloil D	Energol SAE 50
Primary Chaincase	Essolube 20	Castrolite	Shell X-100 20/20 W	Mobiloil Arctic	Energol SAE 20
Telescopic Forks	Essolube 20	Castrolite	Shell X-100 20/20 W	Mobiloil Arctic	Energol SAE 20
Spring-wheel Mechanism (where fitted)	Esso Graphite Grease	Castrolease Graphited or Castrolease Heavy	Shell Retinax A or RB	Mobil Graphited Grease	Energrease C3G
Spring-wheel Ball Bearing (where fitted)	Esso Grease	Castrolease Heavy	Shell Retinax A or RB	Mobilgrease No. 2	Energrease C3
Swinging-fork Spindle	Esso Grease	Castrolease Heavy	Shell Retinax A or RB	Mobilgrease No. 2	Energrease C3
Grease Gun	Esso Grease	Castrolease CL	Shell Retinax A or RB	Mobilgrease No. 2	Energrease C3
Easing Rusted Parts	Esso Penetrating Oil	Castrol Penetrating Oil	Shell Donax P or Retinax A	Mobil Spring Oil	Energol Penetrating Oil

Use a H.M.P. grease in quickly detachable wheel brake-drum bearing.

1,000 miles or every month if this distance has not been covered. The correct quantity is one-third of a pint. The primary chain will be kept in first-class condition and will run for a long mileage without attention, if maintaining the oil level and changing the oil at regular intervals are

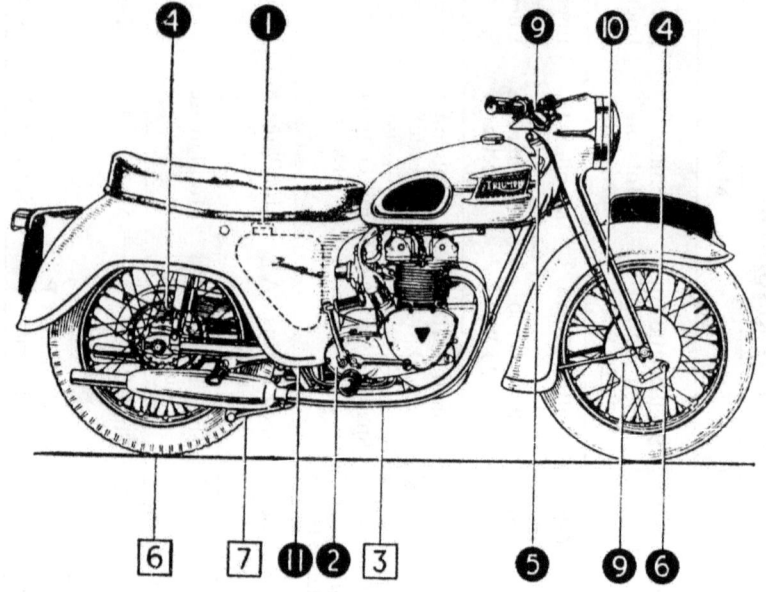

FIG. 19. LUBRICATION CHART (MODELS 3TA AND 5TA)

The numbers in circles refer to the off-side of the motor-cycle. Those in squares refer to the near-side.

No.	Part	S.A.E.	No.	Part	S.A.E.
1.	Engine Oil Tank	20 or 30	7.	Footbrake Pedal Spindle	Grease
2.	Gearbox	50	9.	Exposed Cables	20
3.	Primary Chaincase	20	10.	Fork (hydraulic)	20 or 30
4.	Wheel Hubs	Grease	11.	Swinging Fork Spindle	Grease
5.	Steering Head	Grease		OIL-CAN LUBRICATION All Brake-rod Joints and Pins	20
6.	Brake Cam Spindle	Grease			

attended to as suggested in Chapter VI under "Routine Maintenance after Running-in Period." Neglect will cause rapid chain wear.

GEARBOX. The oil in the gearbox should be drained and the gearbox flushed out after the first 500 miles. Afterwards change the oil every 5,000 miles, but check the oil level at 1,000-mile intervals.

Recommended Lubricants. The various oils and greases recommended by the makers of Triumphs are tabulated on page 41. For 1945–55 machines *summer* grade engine oil, however, is recommended for gearbox lubrication instead of the oils tabulated (for 1956–9 machines). It is, of course, not vital to replenish the gearbox with the gearbox oils recommended on page 41. Summer grade engine oil should be quite suitable. With regard to the gearbox oils tabulated on page 41, note that "Castrol GP" is an abbreviation for "Castrol Grand Prix."

TELESCOPIC FORKS. *See* pages 68–70.
SWINGING ARM. *See* page 87.

CHAPTER IV

LIGHTING AND IGNITION SYSTEMS

On the 1938-9 models 2HC, 3HC Lucas coil-ignition equipment was provided, the dynamo with contact-breaker on the near-side taking the place of the Magdyno which was fitted to earlier models. Automatic voltage control was included on all 1937-9 models, including those with coil ignition. It is also provided on all 1945-59 models fitted with a dynamo, but not on models with a Lucas alternator.

Automatic Voltage Control. Where automatic voltage control is provided (1937 onwards), the cut-out and regulator are combined as a unit separate from the dynamo. The regulator which is connected across the dynamo brushes dispenses with the "third brush" and operates on the "trembler" principle, automatically varying the output of the dynamo according to the state of charge of the battery and the load. Thus, charging is purely automatic and not under the control of the rider.

The Headlamp. The headlamp is fitted with a double-filament bulb; one filament is arranged to be approximately at the focus of the reflector and gives the normal driving light, while the second one, mounted slightly above the other, gives a dipped, anti-dazzling beam for use when meeting traffic or driving in mist or fog, this device being controlled by a switch mounted on the handlebars. A small pilot bulb is also provided for use when the machine is stationary, and for town riding.

The Lighting Switch. The control switch, mounted either at the back of the headlamp or on the instrument panel on 1937-9 models, has the following positions where automatic voltage control is not fitted—

"OFF" Lamps off and dynamo not charging.
"C"   Lamps off and dynamo giving about one-half its normal output.
"H"   Headlamp (main bulb), tail lamp and sidecar lamp, when fitted, on; dynamo giving maximum output.
"L"   The pilot bulb is on and the other lamps are off; dynamo giving maximum output.

Where automatic voltage control is provided (1945–59 magneto models) there are only three switch positions, namely, "OFF," "L," and "H." In all three positions the dynamo gives a controlled output as already explained. During daylight running with the battery well charged the dynamo gives only a trickle charge and the ammeter may show only 1 or 2 amperes.

The Ammeter. This instrument shows the amount of current flowing into or from the battery; it gives an indication that the equipment is working in a satisfactory manner.

THE LUCAS DYNAMO

On models with Lucas dynamo lighting the equipment comprises the following.

Dynamo—Output Control. The dynamo works in conjunction with a regulator unit to give compensated voltage control, but the regulator and cut-out are electrically separate, although combined structurally. Neither should be tampered with as they are both properly adjusted during manufacture.

The regulator provides a completely automatic control. The dynamo output varies according to the load on the battery and its state of charge—the dynamo gives a high output when the battery is discharged, and a trickle-charge only when the battery is fully charged so as to keep the battery in good condition. The regulator also provides increased output when current is taken by the lamps.

The cut-out is an automatic switch. It connects the dynamo to the battery only when the dynamo voltage is higher than the battery voltage, and disconnects to prevent the battery discharging through the dynamo windings.

The dynamo output is correctly set to suit the requirements of the motorcycle and under normal conditions the battery will be kept in good order.

Ammeter Readings. During daytime running, when the battery is in good condition, the dynamo gives only a trickle charge and the ammeter needle shows only a small deflection to the "+" side of the scale.

When the headlamp is switched on, a discharge reading is shown when the battery voltage is high; after a short time the battery voltage drops and the regulator responds so that the dynamo output balances the lamp load.

Lubrication. As grease-packed ball bearings are fitted at both ends, no lubrication is required until the machine is taken down for a general overhaul.

Inspection of Brushgear and Commutator. At six-monthly intervals remove the commutator cover and examine the brushgear and commutator. The brushes—held in boxes by means of springs—must make firm contact with the commutator; see that each brush is free to slide in its holder. If it is sticking, remove and clean with a petrol-moistened cloth. When replacing the brushes each one must be returned to its original position so that it "beds" properly on the commutator. Replace brushes if they are badly worn, but fitting by a Service Agent is desirable to ensure that they "bed" properly on the commutator (see Fig. 20).

To function efficiently the commutator should be free from any trace of oil or dirt and should appear highly polished. If dirty or blackened, clean it by pressing a clean, dry cloth against it while the engine is slowly

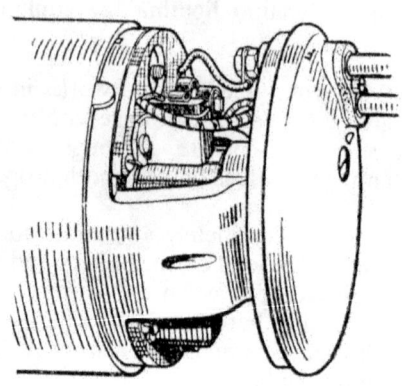

FIG. 20. COMMUTATOR END OF LUCAS DYNAMO WITH COVER BAND REMOVED

turned over by means of the kickstarter; if very dirty, use a petrol-moistened cloth.

THE LUCAS MAGNETO

Where a Triumph is equipped with magneto ignition a rotating-armature pattern magneto is employed. This has the magnet cast into the body; this eliminates joints and improves the weatherproof properties of the magneto. The ignition timing is controlled by a lever on the handlebars.

Lubrication. Lubrication is advised about every 3,000 miles. The cam is supplied with lubricant from a felt pad in a pocket in the contact-breaker housing. A wick in a small hole in the cam allows the oil to find its way to the surface of the cam. To lubricate, remove the contact-breaker cover, turn the engine over until the hole in the cam is seen, then carefully add a few drops of thin machine oil. No oil must be allowed to get on or near the contacts.

The contact-breaker rocker-arm pivot should also be lubricated. The complete contact-breaker must be removed for this purpose. To do this, take out the hexagon-headed screw from the centre of the contact-breaker

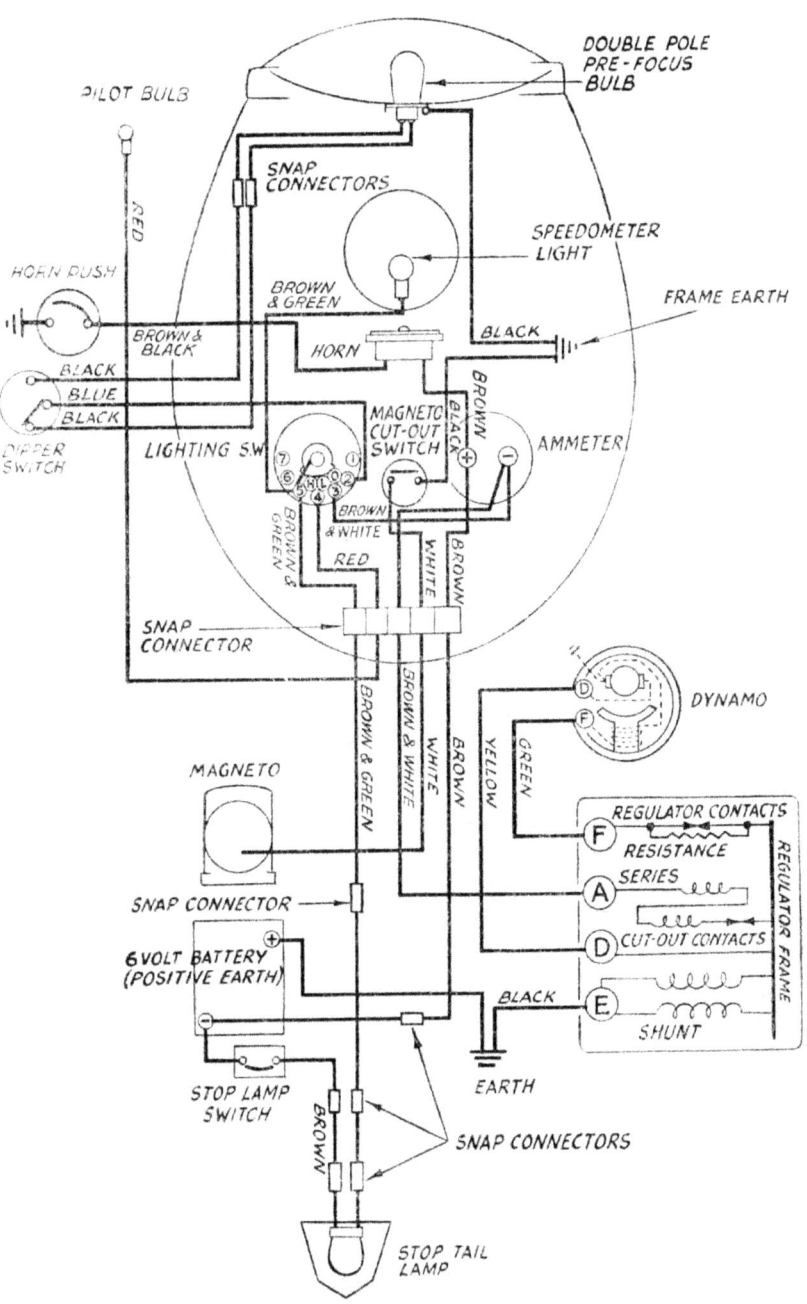

Fig. 21. Wiring Diagram (1945–59 Models with Dynamo)

and lever the contact-breaker carefully off the tapered shaft on which it fits, push aside the rocker-arm retaining spring, lift off the rocker arm and smear the pivot with a little Mobilgrease No. 2.

The cam ring which is a sliding fit in its housing should be removed and the inside and outside surfaces lightly smeared with Mobilgrease No. 2. If the handlebar ignition lever is half retarded, removal and re-fitting the cam is rendered more easy. Apply one or two drops of thin machine-oil to the felt cam-lubricator in the housing. Then re-fit the cam, taking care that the stop peg in the housing and the timing control plunger engage with their respective slots.

In some cases an earthing brush is fitted at the back of the contact-breaker base; see that it is clean and has free movement in its holder before re-fitting. When replacing the contact-breaker, be careful to see that the projecting key on the tapered portion of the contact-breaker case engages with the keyway cut in the magneto spindle. Replace the contact-breaker securing screw and tighten with care, otherwise ignition timing will be affected.

The bearings of the armature are packed with grease by the makers. When the machine is dismantled for general overhaul it is advisable to have the magneto inspected by a Lucas Service Depot or Agent.

Adjustment of Contact-breaker Gap. Check the setting of the contact-breaker every 3,000 miles. To check, remove the contact-breaker cover and turn the engine until the contacts are fully open. A feeler gauge should be used for checking the gap—the gauge should have a thickness of 0·012 in.–0·015 in. (0·30–0·40 mm). A suitable gauge is provided on the magneto spanner. It should be a sliding fit if the gap is correct; adjust the setting if the gap varies appreciably from that recommended. To do this, with the engine in the position which gives maximum separation, slacken the locknut and turn the contact screw by its hexagon head until the gap is properly adjusted. Tighten the locknut and re-check the gap.

Cleaning Contacts. Take off the contact-breaker cover and examine the contact-breaker every 6,000 miles. Clean dirty or pitted contacts with a fine carborundum stone or, if not available, with very fine emery cloth. Wipe away any dirt or metal dust with a petrol-moistened cloth. Remove any rust from the contact-breaker springs. When cleaned, check the contact-breaker gap.

To remove the contacts for cleaning, unscrew the contact-breaker securing screw. Lever the contact-breaker off its tapered shaft, push the locating spring to the side and lift the rocker arm off its pivot; it is then possible to get at the contacts to clean them. Check the projecting key on the tapered portion of the contact-breaker base, when replacing the contact-breaker, to see that it engages with the keyway cut in the armature spindle. Replace the contact-breaker securing screw and tighten carefully.

LIGHTING AND IGNITION SYSTEMS

High-tension Pick-up. Remove this after approximately every 6,000 miles running. Wipe the moulding with a clean, dry cloth, then check that the carbon brush has free movement in its holder, but be careful not to over-stretch the brush spring. Clean the brush if dirty, using a petrol-moistened cloth. A brush worn, say, to within $\frac{1}{8}$ in. (3·0 mm) of the shoulder must be replaced. Before re-fitting the H.T. pick-up, clean the slip-ring track and flanges by pressing a soft, dry cloth on the ring (using a suitably shaped piece of wood) while the engine is turned slowly.

Renewing High-tension Cables. Signs of perishing or cracking in the high-tension cables implies their replacement at once, using 7-mm, rubber-covered ignition cable.

To replace a high-tension cable remove the metal washer and moulded terminal from the defective cable; then thread the new cable through the moulded terminal and cut back the insulation for about $\frac{1}{4}$ in. (6·0 mm), pass the exposed strands through the metal washer and bend them back radially. Finally, screw the terminal into the pick-up moulding.

1937–9 Headlamps. The Lucas DU142, D142 type headlamps are fitted on 1937-9 models. The DU142 and D142 type lamps are similar except that the former is used on models without an instrument panel, while the latter is fitted on machines with an instrument panel. The ammeter and lighting switch are incorporated on the back of the DU142 headlamp.

To focus the main bulb (DU142, D142), first remove the lamp front and reflector by pressing back the fixing clip. Next slacken the clamping screw which secures the bulb-holder and move the holder and bulb until the correct focus is obtained. The clamping screw should afterwards be re-tightened. The bulb-holder may be detached by pressing back the two securing springs. Always locate the top of the rim first when replacing the lamp front and reflector. Bulb replacements are: main bulb, Lucas No. 168; parking bulb, Lucas No. 200.

LUCAS RM14 AND RM15 A.C. LIGHTING AND IGNITION

General Description. Electrical energy in the form of rectified A.C. passes through the battery from the alternator, the rate of charge depending on the position of the lighting switch. During daytime running, the alternator output is sufficient only to supply the ignition coil and to trickle-charge the battery. When the lighting switch is turned to "Pilot" or "Head" ("P" and "H") positions the output increases proportionately.

Under "Emergency" starting conditions, trickle-charging continues while an ignition performance, similar to that from a magneto, is obtained. It is of paramount importance to remember the following: After the engine has been started, normal running is resumed by turning the ignition key from "EMG" to "IGN." If the battery must be removed, the engine can be run with the ignition switch in the "EMG" position, provided that the battery negative cable (brown) is earthed to the frame. Under these conditions no lighting is available.

Circuit Details. The alternator stator carries three pairs of series-connected coils (*see* Figs. 22 and 23), one pair being permanently connected across the rectifier bridge network. The latter pair provide some degree of charging current for the battery whenever the engine is running.

Connexions to the remaining coil vary according to the positions of the lighting and ignition controls. The alternator output from the battery-charging coils is regulated to the minimum by interaction of the rotor flux set up by the current flowing in the short-circuited coils during daylight running. In the "Pilot" position these latter coils are disconnected and the regulating fluxes are reduced; the alternator output, therefore, increases and compensates for the extra parking-light load. The alternator output is further increased in the "Head" position by the connexion of all three pairs of coils in parallel.

Emergency Starting (Ignition Switch at "EMG"). With this circuit the contact-breaker opens when the alternating current in the windings reaches the maximum. When current flows and the contacts are closed, the main circuit to the alternator is through one arm of the rectifier bridge. At the moment of contact separation, the built-up energy of the alternator windings quickly discharges through an alternative circuit provided by the battery and the ignition coil primary windings; this rapid transfer of energy from alternator to coil causes H.T. to be induced in the ignition coil secondary winding and a spark to occur at the plug.

Since, when the engine is running and the ignition switch is at "EMG," the battery receives a charging current, so the battery voltage begins to rise. This rising voltage opposes the alternator voltage, gradually bringing about a reduction in the energy available to the coil. This reduction in energy, owing to the misfiring which results, will remind the rider to switch over to normal running.

Construction. The alternator consists of a spigot-mounted and bolted 6-coil laminated stator with the centre-bored rotor carried on, and driven by, an extension to the crankshaft. The rotor has a hexagonal steel core, each face of which carries a high-energy permanent magnet keyed to a laminated pole-tip. The pole tips are riveted to brass side plates, the assembly being cast in aluminium and machined to give a smooth external finish. The stator and rotor can be separated without the need arising to fit magnet keepers to the rotor poles.

The alternator is designed for use with headlamp bulbs not exceeding 30-watts rating.

Fig. 22. Primary Chaincase Cover Removed to Show Rotor and Stator

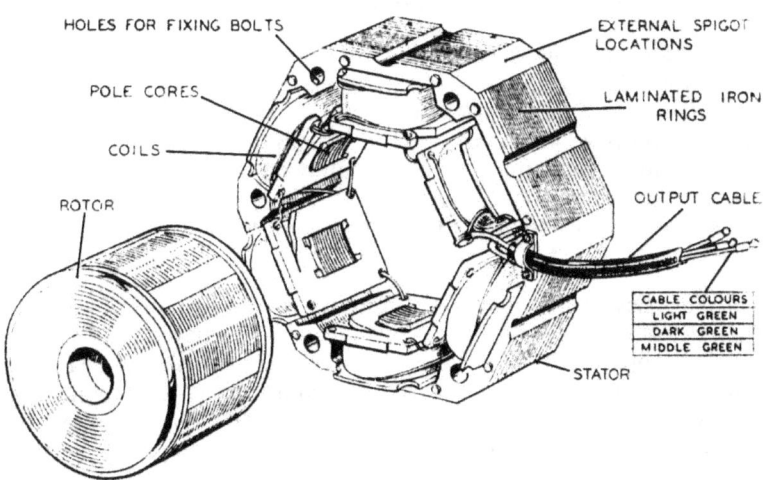

Fig. 23. Alternator (Model R.M. 14)

The Alternator. The alternator requires no attention except for occasional inspection of the snap-connectors in the three green output cables (*see* Fig. 23). These must be kept clean and tight.

The Lucas Rectifier. The rectifier comprises four plates (coated on one side with selenium) and operates like a non-return valve; it allows current to pass in *one direction* only. The alternating current from the Lucas alternator is thereby converted to unidirectional (d.c.) current for charging the battery.

The rectifier does not require any maintenance except to see that the connexions (*see* Fig. 24) are kept tight and clean, and to check periodically that the nut which secures the rectifier to the frame is quite tight. *On no account loosen the nut which clamps the rectifier plates together.* This nut is most carefully adjusted during the original assembly of the rectifier. Slackening it can affect the proper functioning of the unit.

FIG. 24. THE LUCAS RECTIFIER SHOWING CONNEXION POINTS

The Lucas Battery. This, of course, is concerned with both lighting and ignition. It must be regularly attended to. Battery maintenance is dealt with on pages 59–61.

Ignition Coil. Keep the ignition coil clean, particularly between the terminals, and the terminal connexions tight.

Lubrication of Contact-breaker (Distributor DKX2A). Lubricate this unit (*see* Fig. 26) every 5,000 miles. Remove the metal cover and smear the face of the cam lightly with one of the greases recommended for the grease gun on page 41. If this is not available, clean engine oil may be used. On no account must grease be allowed to get on to or near the contacts.

Lubricate the automatic timing control mechanism, using a thin machine-oil.

Cleaning Distributor DKX2A. Remove the distributor cover every 6,000 miles, and wipe it inside and outside with a clean, dry, fluffless cloth. The contact-breaker should be examined; the contacts should be free from grease or oil. Clean with a fine carborundum stone or very fine emery cloth if burned or blackened, then wipe away any dirt or metal dust with a clean petrol-moistened cloth.

Contact-breaker Gap (Distributor DKX2A). This should be checked after the first 500 miles and afterwards every 3,000 miles. To check, remove the sparking plugs and turn the engine over slowly until the

LIGHTING AND IGNITION SYSTEMS 53

contacts are fully open, then insert a 0·014 in.–0·016 in. (0·36–0·4 mm) feeler gauge between the contacts. The gauge will be a sliding fit if the gap is correct. Any appreciable variation from the gauge thickness means

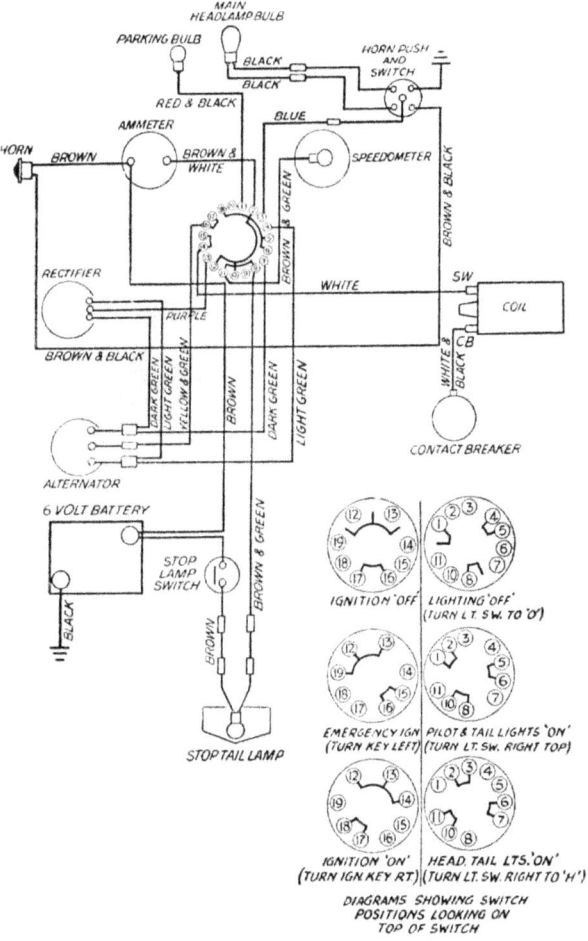

Fig. 25. Wiring Diagram (5T, 6T, 3TA and 5TA)

adjusting the setting. To adjust, if necessary, keep the engine in the position which gives maximum contact opening, and slacken the screw at the side of the body unit; then slide the fixed contact carrier into its slotted hole until the correct gap is obtained. Re-tighten the screw.

The easiest way to clean the contact-breaker is first to take off the moving contact. To do this, unscrew the nut securing the end of the spring (*see* Fig. 26) and withdraw the spring washer, spring, and bush. Clean the pivot pin and smear it very lightly with some clean engine oil before replacing the moving contact and spring.

Lubrication and Cleaning of Contact-breaker (Distributor 18D2). In the case of models 3TA and 5TA these operations should be attended to about every 5,000 miles. Withdraw and clean the distributor cover inside and outside. Direct special attention to the spaces between the metal

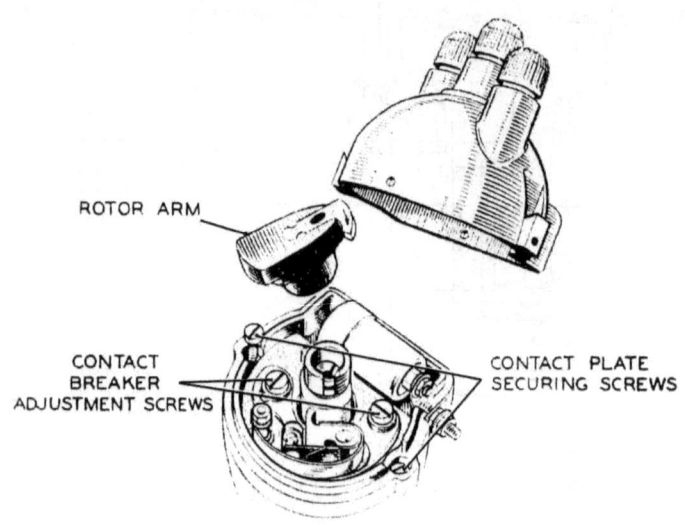

FIG. 26. DISTRIBUTOR (MODEL DKX2A WITH COVER REMOVED)
Fitted to all 1945-59 models except models 3TA and 5TA.

electrodes in the cover, and see that the small carbon brush moves freely in its holder.

Lift off the rotor arm (*see* Fig. 27), and unscrew the two screws which secure the contact-breaker base plate. Then remove the base plate and lubricate the automatic ignition-advance mechanism with some clean engine oil; pay special attention to the pivots. Replace the base plate and the rotor arm.

Inspect the contact-breaker closely. Both contacts should be free from oil or grease. If the contacts are blackened or burned, clean them with a slip of fine carborundum stone or with some *very fine* emery cloth. Afterwards with a clean petrol-moistened cloth wipe away any traces of metal dust or dirt. The proper cleaning of the two contacts is much simplified by first removing the contact-breaker lever which carries the moving contact. Lightly smear the cam and pivot post with a little Mobilgrease No. 2 or clean engine oil before replacing the contact-breaker lever. But be most careful not to allow any oil or grease to get on or close to the

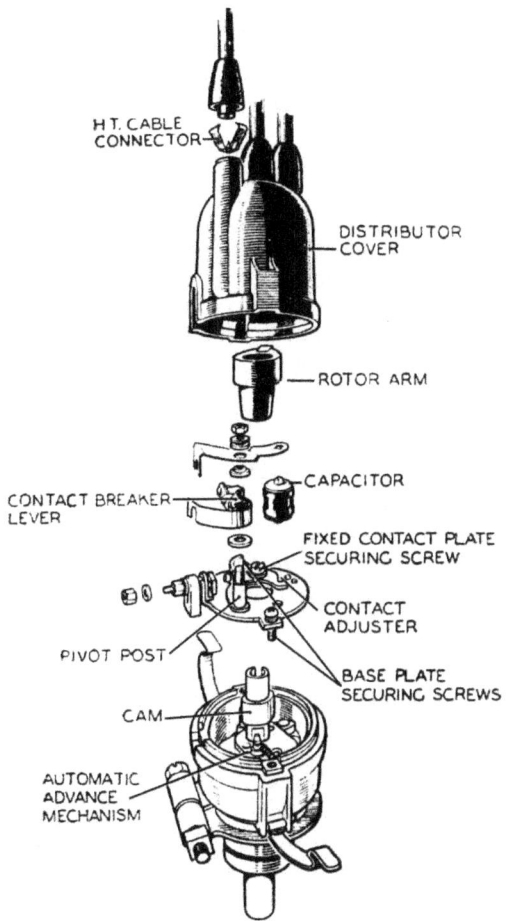

Fig. 27. Distributor (Model 18D2) Shown Dismantled
Fitted to models 3TA and 5TA.

actual contacts. This is most important. Having cleaned the distributor unit and the contacts, check the gap between the contacts.

Contact-breaker Gap (Distributor 18D2). Check the gap on a new model 3TA or 5TA after covering 500 miles, and subsequently about every 3,000 miles. To check the contact-breaker gap, remove both sparking plugs and turn the engine over slowly until the contacts are seen to be wide open. Then insert a suitable gauge between the contacts. If the gap is correct, the gauge should be a nice sliding fit between them. The correct gap is 0·014 in.- 0·016 in.

Where a gap adjustment is called for, keep the engine in the position which causes full opening of the contacts and loosen the screw which secures the fixed contact plate. Insert a screwdriver between the two studs on the base plate and the notch in the fixed contact plate, and adjust the position of the plate until the correct gap is obtained between the contacts. Afterwards tighten the securing screw and again check that the gap is correct.

High-tension Cables. Replace the high-tension cables if they show signs of perishing or cracking, using a 7-mm, P.V.C.- or Neoprene-covered ignition cable. This is easily done by removing the metal washer and moulded nut from the defective cable. Then thread the new cable through the moulded nut and bare the conductor for about ¼ in. Pass the exposed strands through the metal washer and bend back the strands radially. Finally, re-fit the moulded nut into the H.T. terminal.

LUCAS LAMPS (1945–59 MODELS)

The lamps fitted to the majority of the 1945–59 models have a double-filament, pre-focus, 6-volt 30/24-watt, Lucas No. 373 or 312 bulb. In the case of the TR5 models, they are fitted with a double-filament, 6-volt 30/30-watt, Lucas bulb (not pre-focused) and a 6-volt 3-watt Lucas No. 988 pilot bulb.

Replacing the Headlamp Bulb—Nacelle Type. Access to the headlamp bulb is gained by slackening the front rim retaining screw located at the top of the lamp fixing ring. Disengage and withdraw the front rim and light unit assembly, after removing the upper edge. Press the moulded adapter inwards and turn it to the left. Lift off the adaptor and withdraw the bulb. When fitting the replacement bulb, locate the slot in the bulb flange with the projection in the bulb holder; re-fit the adaptor, engaging its moulded recesses with the corresponding projections on the bulb holder, then press inwards and secure by turning the adaptor to the right.

To gain access to the bulbs on pre-1956 model TR5, release the catch at the base of the lamp and then the rim and reflector assembly can be removed from the shell. The focusing of the main bulb is made by slackening the holder clip screw and moving the bulb holder in or out as necessary. When replacing the reflector rim assembly, first fit the reflector to the shell and locate with the rubber head; assemble the rim and glass, engaging the tongue into the top of the shell and the fastener catch into the rim.

Setting the Headlamp Beam. Place the machine in front of a light coloured wall at a distance of about 25 feet when setting the headlamp

LIGHTING AND IGNITION SYSTEMS

beam. During this check, the motor-cycle should be carrying its normal load, as the rider's weight (and that of a pillion passenger) is liable to affect the setting. Switch on the main beam, directing this straight ahead and parallel with the ground. If this direction is not obtained, loosen the two small screws on each side of the lamp fixing ring and raise or lower the beam by pulling-out or pressing-in the bottom of the ring. On some "Trophy" models (without nacelle headlamp) to adjust the beam, slacken the two headlamp securing bolts and tilt the headlamp as required. When the required beam has been obtained, re-tighten the two screws.

If the Lucas pre-focus type bulb is fitted, the filament is correctly positioned during manufacture in relation to the focal point of the reflector, so no further focusing is necessary.

Parking Lamp. This lamp is fitted with a 6-volt 3-watt Lucas No. 988 bulb. Replacement of the bulb is simple; just unscrew the two screws on the sides of the rim and remove the rim and glass. The bulb can then be taken out by pressing it in and turning it to the left. Put in the new bulb and replace the rim and glass in the reverse order to removal.

Rear Lamp. Remove the two moulded retaining screws to gain access to the rear light bulbs. The correct replacement for the stop tail lamp is a Lucas No. 384 6-volt 6/18-watt bulb. This bulb has offset securing pins to prevent incorrect insertion into the bulb holder and to ensure that the higher wattage filament is illuminated when the brake pedal is depressed. Should the 6-watt filament fail, do not change the cables over to obtain rear lighting from the 18-watt filament as the heat generated is liable to burn the plastics lens.

Headlamp and Top Nacelle Unit. *Removal (Dynamo-equipped Models).* Disconnect the battery positive lead. Unscrew and remove the steering damper.

Headlamp. Unscrew the retaining screw at the top of the headlamp retaining ring and ease the headlamp away from the ring, pulling from the top. Disconnect the earth wire (black) from the bulb holder frame and the two headlamp leads (black) at the snap connectors.

Retaining Ring. Remove by unscrewing the two small screws at the sides of the ring.

Motifs. Unscrew the four screws and two nuts securing the motifs and remove.

Rear Nacelle Retaining Screws. Remove the two small screws and nuts holding the rear of the top unit to the fork covers.

Five Point Connector. Disconnect all leads at the connector. Leave the connector in position on the stanchion, if the top unit only is being removed. If the fork assembly is to be removed, take the connector from the stanchion and disconnect the leads so that the connector remains with the top unit.

Speedometer. Unscrew the speedometer-drive cable at the head.
Horn. Disconnect both leads.
Dipswitch Lead to Light Switch. This should be disconnected at the light switch (No. 2 position).
Assembly. Reassemble in the reverse order.

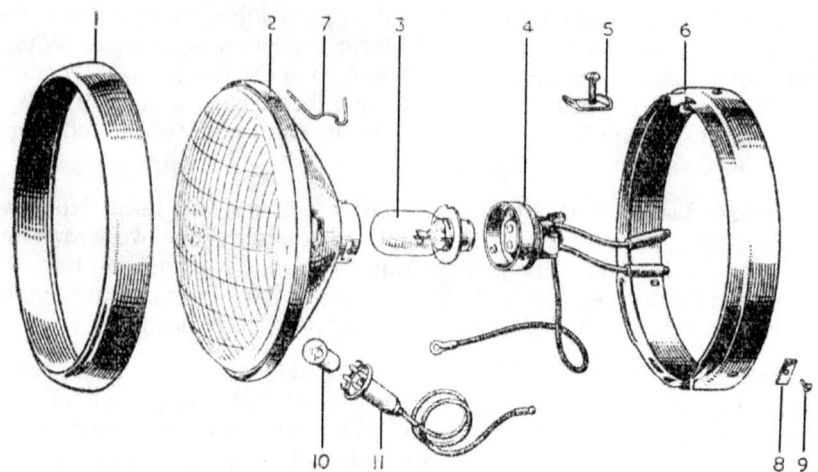

FIG. 28. SHOWING DETAILS OF LUCAS TRIUMPH HEADLAMP

The headlamp illustrated is provided on all 1945-59 machines except the Trophy TR5 models.

1. Front rim
2. The light-unit
3. Pre-focus 30/24 W main bulb
4. Main bulb adaptor
5. Plate securing 1
6. Lamp fixing ring
7. Wire clip
8. Tapped plate
9. Screw for 8
10. 3 W pilot bulb
11. Pilot bulb holder

Removal (A.C.-equipped Models). Dismantle as for "Dynamo-equipped Models" to "Rear Nacelle Retaining Screws" and then proceed as follows—

Lighting and Ignition Switch. There is a small grub screw at the side of the plastic switch lever and this should be unscrewed; then pull the lever away from the switch. Then unscrew the brass nut around the switch body and remove the name disc. Unscrew the two screws which retain the switch to the nacelle and push the switch through into the nacelle.

Horn. Disconnect the black lead from the horn terminal.

Speedometer. The speedometer-drive cable at the head should be unscrewed, when the speedometer light can be detached.

Ammeter. The brown leads at the ammeter should be disconnected; one from the left-hand terminal and two from the right-hand terminal.

If the top unit only is to be removed, it is unnecessary to proceed any further. If, however, the forks are to be removed, disconnect the blue lead from the dipper switch to switch position No. 3, and also the red and black pilot light lead. Snap connectors are fitted to both these leads.

Assembly. Reassemble in reverse order.

BATTERY MAINTENANCE

Water is lost by gassing and evaporation during charging, and to maintain the battery in a healthy condition the water must be replaced.

Topping-up. The electrolyte (acid solution) level in the cells of the battery must be maintained, so once a month (more often in very hot

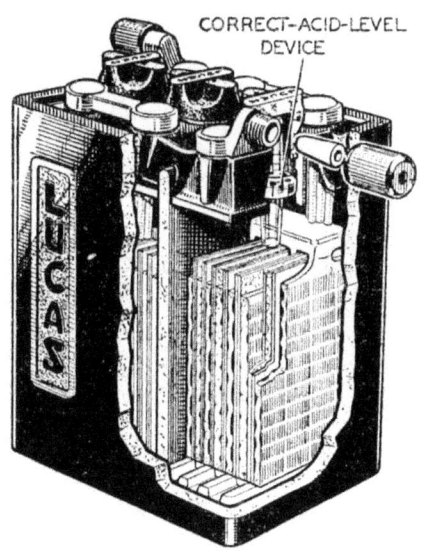

FIG. 29. LUCAS BATTERY MODEL PU7E/9
Showing correct acid-level device and detachable cable connectors.
This battery is fitted to all 1945–59 models.

weather) this should be examined. If required, *distilled* water must be added to bring the electrolyte just level with the top of the separators.

A naked light must not be used when examining the condition of the cells, as there is a risk of igniting the gas coming from the active materials.

The correct acid solution level device consists of a central tube with a perforated flange which rests on a ledge in the filling orifice (*see* Fig. 29). When topping-up a battery fitted with these devices, pour distilled water around the flange (not down the tube) until no more drains through into the cell. This happens when the electrolyte level reaches the bottom of the central tube and so prevents further escape of the air displaced by topping-up with water. If the tube is then lifted slightly, the small amount of water in the flange will drain into the cell and the acid solution level will be correct.

Checking Battery Condition. Now and again the condition of the battery should be checked by taking measurements of the specific gravity of the electrolyte in each of the cells. A small volume hydrometer (*see* Fig. 30) should be used for this purpose—this resembles a syringe containing

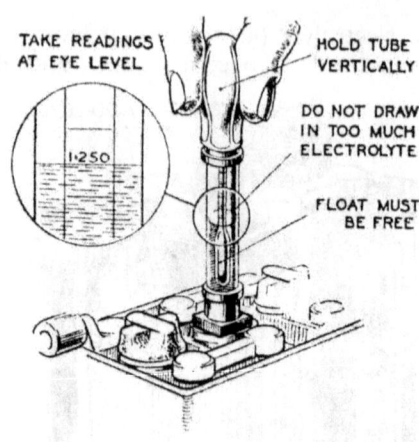

FIG. 30. CHECKING SPECIFIC GRAVITY WITH LUCAS HYDROMETER

a graduated float which indicates the specific gravity of the acid solution in the cell from which the sample is taken. Note that measurements should not be taken directly after the cells have been topped-up, as at this time the electrolyte is not thoroughly mixed.

Tilt the battery so that sufficient electrolyte is above the separators before taking a sample. This is necessary because the space between each separator is not wide enough to allow the nozzle of the hydrometer to be inserted.

The indications of the specific gravity readings are—

1·280–1·300	Cell fully charged
About 1·210	Cell about half discharged
Below 1·150	Cell fully discharged

The reading for each cell should be approximately the same. If one cell, however, gives a very different value from the rest, the battery should be examined by a Lucas Service Depot* or Agent, as it shows that acid has

---

* The London depots are at Dordrecht Road, Acton Vale, W.4, and at 757–759 High Road, Leyton, E.10.

been spilled or has leaked from the cell in question or there may be a short circuit between the plates.

The battery must not be left in a discharged condition. Should the machine be out of use for any length of time, have the battery fully charged and every two weeks have it given a short refreshing charge, so as to prevent any likelihood of the plates becoming permanently sulphated.

Detachable Cable Connectors. When connecting the battery, unscrew the knurled nut and withdraw the collet or cone-shaped insert. Remember this is not interchangeable with the collet in the other terminal. Bare the end of the cable about one inch and thread one bared end through the knurled nut and collet; then bend back the cable strands over the narrow end of the collet and insert the collet and cable into the terminal block. Tighten the knurled nut to secure the connexion.

Battery Earth. The a.c. Lighting-ignition Unit and dynamo are designed for positive (+) earth systems. Reversal of the battery connexions will cause serious damage.

THE HORN

The electric horns fitted to Triumph motor-cycles are adjusted to give their best performance before being passed out of the works; they give a long period of service without attention.

Should the action of the horn become uncertain—emitting a choking sound only—it is not proof that it has broken down. It is possible the trouble is due to some outside source—a discharged battery, a loose connexion, or short-circuit in the wiring of the horn, or the horn-push bracket may not be in good electrical contact with the handlebar. It is also on the cards that the horn's performance is upset by loose mounting.

The tone of the horn is not altered if the following adjustment be made, for it is designed to take up any wear of the moving parts which, if not corrected, results in loss of power and roughness of note. Accurate adjustment requires the use of a 10-amp d.c. ammeter—the highest permissible current consumption is 6 amperes at 6 volts—but as the owner of the machine is hardly likely to own one of these instruments, he can carry out the following if he considers that the note of the horn has deteriorated considerably. Operate the horn-push and turn the adjustment screw anti-clockwise until the horn just fails to sound, release the horn-push and turn the adjustment screw clockwise for a quarter of a turn (six notches) when the original performance should be restored. Turn the screw one notch at a time if further adjustment is necessary. If the original performance cannot be restored, however, the horn should be sent to a Lucas Service Depot for attention.

SPARKING PLUGS

Suitable Sparking Plugs. Always run on a sparking plug suitable for the particular machine concerned, and recommended by the engine manufacturers. Three very reliable types of sparking plugs are the Lodge, the K.L.G., and the Champion. Waterproof terminal covers and watertight plugs corresponding to the standard types are also available if desired.

All Triumph twin-cylinder engines require sparking plugs with a 14-mm thread and on all except a few types the correct plug reach is ½ in. On some earlier engines and those with a light-alloy cylinder head the correct plug reach is ⅜ in. Where a plug with ½ in. reach is required, suitable types are the Lodge HN or H14, the K.L.G. F70, and the Champion L10S. Where a plug with ¾ in. reach is required, suitable types are the Lodge HLN, the K.L.G. FE70, and the Champion NA8. For most

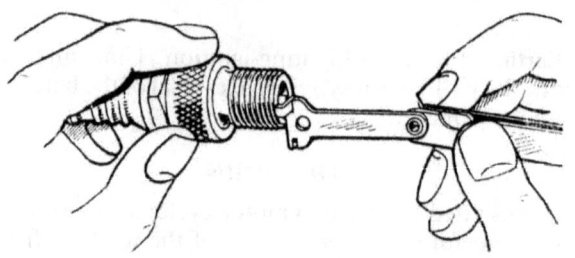

FIG. 31. A SAFE METHOD OF RE-GAPPING A PLUG
The Champion tool shown includes suitable gauges

recent engines suitable alternative plugs to the Lodge HLN are the K.L.G. FE75 and the Champion N3. The K.L.G. FE100 is, however, recommended instead of the K.L.G. FE75 for recent models TR5, TR6, T100 and T120. On no account fit a short reach plug where a long reach type is required, and *vice versa*.

Correct Sparking Plug Gap. Difficult starting or occasional misfiring can usually be traced to a dirty or unserviceable sparking plug. The life of a good plug is considerable, but the points of the electrodes gradually burn away and eventually the gap becomes too large and it is necessary to reset the points.

It is advisable to check the plug gap regularly (say every 2,500 miles) and to adjust the gap on "Magdyno" models if burning of the points has caused the gap to exceed the maximum correct gap. The makers of Triumphs recommend a gap 0·016 in.–0·018 in. and 0·018 in.–0·020 in. for magneto and coil-ignition models respectively. It is preferable to use gaps of 0·018 in. and 0·020 in. Check the gap with a suitable feeler gauge. The gauge should just enter without springing the points.

When adjusting the plug gap, never attempt to bend or tap the *centre* electrode. Use a pair of snipe-nose pliers, or a plug re-gapping tool (shown in Fig. 31), to bend the outside (earth) electrode(s). Tapping the earth electrode(s) is not a good method. When the plug has to be thoroughly cleaned, this should be done as described below, and the plug re-gapped *afterwards*.

Plug Examination. When a plug has been removed the condition of the insulator should be examined. If it is *light brown*, it shows that the mixture strength is correct and that the engine is running at the correct temperature; if it is *dull black*, it proves that the plug is running too cold and, therefore, the carbon is not burned, this being the result of running on a too-rich mixture or of the engine's being left running with too liberal a slow-running setting; if the insulator is *ash white*, it indicates that the plug is over-heating, the usual cause being that the mixture is too weak or that the ignition is retarded too much.

Cleaning a Sparking Plug. If carburation is correct and excessive oil is not entering the combustion chamber, it should not be necessary to dismantle and clean the sparking plug thoroughly more often than once about every 3,000 miles. When running-in a new or rebored engine, it is advisable to remove and check the plug for cleanliness at intervals of about 500 miles.

Quick cleaning of a plug can be done by brushing the points and slightly rubbing their firing sides with smooth emery-cloth. Alternatively the plug can be cleaned with a proprietary gadget. Thorough cleaning (internal and external), however, is not possible without dismantling the plug.

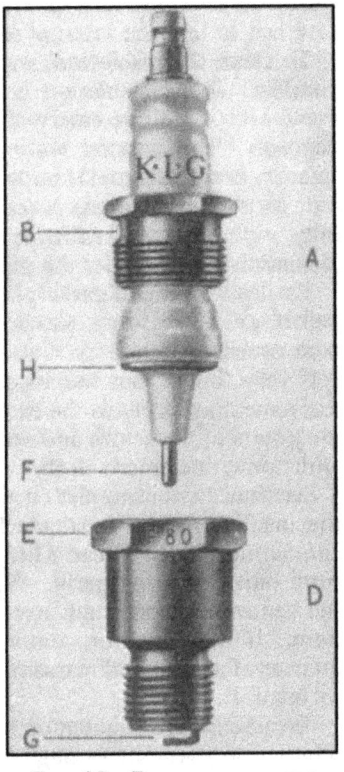

FIG. 32. DETACHABLE-TYPE SPARKING PLUG (K.L.G.) DISMANTLED FOR THOROUGH CLEANING

The gland nut *B* and the internal washer *H* are shown still in position on the insulation.

To Clean K.L.G. and Lodge Plugs Thoroughly. Fig. 32 shows a typical detachable type (K.L.G.) sparking plug dismantled for thorough cleaning. To dismantle a detachable-type sparking plug, hold the smaller hexagon of the gland nut (*B*) lightly in a vice or with a suitable spanner. If you use a vice, be most careful not to exert any pressure on the hexagon faces. Then with a suitable box spanner applied to the larger hexagon (*E*) of the plug body, unscrew the body until it is separated from the gland nut.* The centre electrode (*F*) with its insulation (comprising the insulated electrode assembly (*A*)) can now be detached from the gland nut. Take care not to lose the internal sealing washer (*H*).

To clean the insulation, wipe it clean with a cloth soaked in petrol or paraffin. If the insulation is coated with hard-carbon deposits, remove these with some fine emery-cloth, but make no attempt to scrape off the deposits. The internal sealing washer (*H*) and the surfaces on the insulator, and in the metal body on which this washer rests, are very important as they prevent gas leakage through the plug. Therefore wipe them only with a rag soaked in petrol or paraffin. Any damage caused while dismantling will render the plug unserviceable.

To clean the metal parts (plug body and gland nut) wipe them clean with petrol, or, if necessary, scrape off the deposits with a small knife, or use a wire brush. Afterwards rinse the parts in petrol. The gland nut seldom gets very fouled, but the inside of the plug body may be very dirty, and the same may apply to the external threads of the plug. Clean and polish the points of the centre and outside (earth) electrodes (*F*) and (*G*) (Fig. 32) with some fine emery cloth.

See that there is no dirt or grit lodged between the body of the plug and the insulation, and particularly on the internal sealing washer and the contacting faces. Smear a little thin oil on the internal washer and make sure that it seats properly. When assembling the sparking plug, see that the centre electrode and insulation are positioned centrally in the body bore. If they are not, remove, re-position by rotating assembly (*A*) a quarter of a turn, and reassemble. Do not attempt to force it into position or bend it.

Avoid excessive tightening of the gland nut (*B*). Finally verify that the plug gap is correct (*see* page 62).

Cleaning Champion Plugs. To clean a non-detachable type Champion plug, take it to the nearest garage equipped with a Champion Service Unit. With this apparatus the plug can be cleaned of all deposits in a few minutes, washed, subjected to a high-pressure air line, and afterwards tested for sparking on the Champion apparatus at an air pressure of over 100 lb per sq in.

Replacing the Plug. Before replacing a plug, renew the copper washer if it is worn or flattened, and clean the plug threads with a wire brush.

* Where a detachable-type sparking plug has been in service for a very considerable time, the plug may be found extremely difficult to dismantle, in which case the attempt should be abandoned.

LIGHTING AND IGNITION SYSTEMS

Screw the plug home by hand as far as possible, and always use the plug spanner for final tightening.

When replacing a sparking plug on a light-alloy cylinder head, smear the threads with graphite and do not over-tighten or difficulty may be experienced in removing the plug after carbon has been deposited around the threads.

CHECKING ELECTRICAL CONNEXIONS

Before an attempt is made to diagnose an ignition fault it is suggested that the rider should check all electrical connexions, cleaning and tightening them if necessary.

Engine Will Not Start. NO SPARK AT PLUGS. To check, take out the plugs and put them on the cylinder head, re-fitting the connector. Turn the ignition switch to "IGN" and kick over the engine; a blue spark should be seen at the plug points, but if there is no spark, turn the switch to "EMG" and test again.

Oiled, Fouled or Faulty Plugs. Clean plugs, preferably in an "Air Blast" unit; re-set points and re-fit. If faulty, replace with a correct type plug.

Distributor. See that the cover is fitting properly and that the clips are secure. Check contact-breaker points and clean and adjust them if necessary.

Coil. Clean the extension of the coil, particularly between the cable connexions. Connect a volt-meter between the coil terminal marked "SW" and earth to check the low-tension circuit. No reading with the ignition switch on indicates a fault in the primary coil winding. If the low-tension primary circuit is in order, remove the coil H.T. lead from the distributor cover; remove the cover and rotate the engine until the contact points are closed; switch on the ignition and hold the end of the H.T. lead about $\frac{1}{4}$ in. (6 mm) from the cylinder block; then flick the contact points open with a finger and a spark should pass to the cylinder block. If there is no spark, a fault in the coil H.T. winding is indicated. A coil fault can be corrected only by fitting a new unit.

Engine Will Not Start on "IGN," but Will on "EMG." Causes—discharged battery due to a short circuit; poor condition of the battery owing to age or damage; prolonged use for parking or a low rate of charge from the alternator. Have the battery charged from an external source and the equipment examined by an authorized Lucas Agent or Triumph Dealer.

Engine Runs on "IGN," but Not on "EMG." Leads and connexions from ignition switch to coil and from coil to distributor should be examined. Check distributor contacts and ignition timing (*see* pages 52 and 101). If the engine will still not run on "EMG," have the equipment checked by an authorized Lucas agent or Triumph dealer.

Rough Running and Misfiring on "IGN." Check earth connexions for battery and rectifier and the wiring of the switch and rectifier.

CLEANING

Cleanliness is Important. Keep your mount nice and clean. Doubtless it costs quite a sum, and it is well worth careful looking after. With regular and proper cleaning it will function better, will last longer, maintain its good looks, and retain a good market value. A dirty motor-cycle is an eyesore, and remember that dirt hides defects, encourages rusting, and is a menace when stripping down. Never leave your Triumph Twin soaking wet overnight. If you have no time for cleaning in wet weather, grease the machine all over *before* use.

Cleaning the Engine and Gearbox. See that the cylinder barrel and cylinder-head fins are kept clean and black (except aluminium alloy heads). If the enamel has worn away, paint the fins with some proprietary cylinder black after thorough cleaning with a stiff brush dipped in paraffin. Note that rusted fins, besides looking shabby, cause an appreciable loss in heat dispersion.

Scour off all filth from the lower part of the engine and gearbox with stiff brushes and paraffin. Clean all aluminium alloy and bright surfaces first with a rag damped in paraffin, assisted by brushes where necessary, and then with a dry rag.

Cleaning the Enamel. Never attempt to remove mud from the enamelled parts when dry and caked, as this is likely to damage the surfaces. Soak the mud off with a hose if available. In the case of a very dirty machine it may be advisable to paint the surfaces over with a cleaning compound such as "Gunk" before directing a stream of water on to the dirty surfaces. Be careful not to allow any water to get on the wheel-hub bearings and the magneto or distributor and coil and carburettor. If a hose is not available, soak the mud and then disperse it with plenty of clean water, using a sponge and pail.

Having removed all dirt, dry the enamelled surfaces with a chamois leather and afterwards polish them with soft dusters and some good wax polish or a proprietary polish such as "Karpol."

"Dry weather" riders can keep a machine in almost showroom condition merely by rubbing the enamel over with a paraffin-damped rag, followed by a dry, soft duster.

Cleaning the Chromium. Never employ liquid metal polish or paste, as this will wear down the thin surface. A good chromium-cleaning compound can, however, safely be used, though too frequent use is not desirable. The normal method of removing tarnish (salt deposits) is to clean the surfaces regularly with a damp chamois leather and then polish them with soft dusters.

To Reduce Tarnishing. During the winter months it is a good plan to wipe over occasionally all chromium surfaces with a soft cloth soaked in a proprietary anti-tarnish preparation. An example is "Tekall," obtainable in ½-pint and 1-pint tins.

CHAPTER V

GENERAL MAINTENANCE: THE MOTOR-CYCLE

ADJUSTMENT, lubrication and cleaning of the motor-cycle parts are essential to the smooth running of the machine as a whole. For advice on lubrication and the lighting system, *see* Chapters III and IV. *See also* the Appendix.

FORKS AND STEERING HEAD

Front Forks (1937–9). End play should be taken up in the fork spindles as soon as it is detected because play affects the steering and also the action of the shock-absorbers. On new machines the spindle bearings and shock-absorbers settle down after about 1,000 miles, and therefore at the end of this period and subsequently about every 2,000 miles the front forks should be examined for spindle play. The correct adjustment of the spindles is such that the knurled-edge washers are just free to spin. There should be no general looseness. To adjust each spindle, loosen the end nuts and then turn with a spanner the squared end until the above-mentioned adjustment is obtained. Re-tighten the locknuts and again check the adjustment.

The Triumph Telescopic Forks (1945–59). The improved Triumph telescopic fork, as incorporated in the 1945–59 models, with six inches of hydraulically damped movement, sets a high standard of controllability and comfort. Fig. 33 shows the internal arrangement. The long supple fork springs are enclosed inside the stanchions, and this enables these latter vital components to be of maximum possible diameter and strength. No adjustments of any kind have to be made by the rider, and maintenance is reduced to checking all external nuts, screws and washers. During normal service there is no need to top-up the forks with oil, as the fork action is not affected even if there has been slight leakage. Every 5,000 miles draining and re-filling should be carried out, but if leakage becomes excessive it will be necessary to drain and re-fill the forks before this distance has been covered.

DRAINING. To drain, remove the two drain plugs (18, Fig. 33) at the base of the bottom cover tubes and compress the forks a few times; this causes the oil to drain out more rapidly.

RE-FILLING. Replace the drain plugs; remove the headlamp rim assembly from the nacelle so that the upper parts of the stanchions (27, Fig. 33) are exposed; unscrew the two screwed oil-plugs in the stanchions

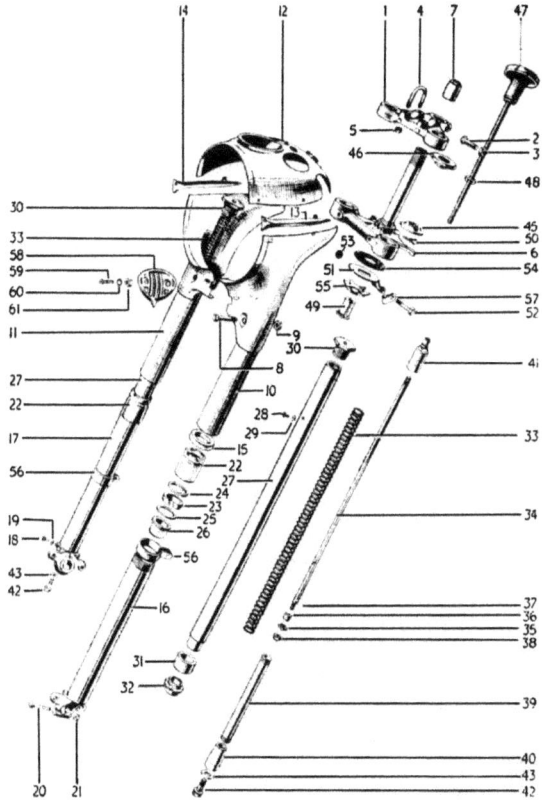

FIG. 33. 1945-55 TELESCOPIC FORKS (1956-9: *see* FIG. 34)

1. Fork head lug
2. Pinch-bolt
3. Nut
4. "U"-bolt
5. Nut
6. Crown and stem
7. Sleeve nut
8. Pinch-bolt
9. Stop nut
10. Nacelle cover, N.S.
11. Nacelle cover, O.S.
12. Nacelle top
13. Motif, N.S.
14. Motif, O.S.
15. Felt washer
16. Bottom tube cover, N.S.
17. Bottom tube cover, O.S.
18. Drain plug
19. Washer
20. Wheel lug pinch-bolt
21. Nut
22. Dust excluder sleeve
23. Felt washer
24. Washer
25. Washer
26. Upper bearing
27. Stanchion
28. Oil filler plug
29. Washer
30. Cap nut
31. Lower stanchion bearing
32. Hydraulic-stop nut
33. Fork spring
34. Oil restrictor rod
35. Oil restrictor
36. Cup
37. Cup pin
38. Nut
39. Pressure tube
40. Pressure tube body
41. Pressure tube sleeve
42. Bolt
43. Copper washer
45. Cone
46. Cone and dust cover
47. Damper assy. knob
48. Damper washer
49. Sleeve
50. Securing pin
51. Damper anchor plate
52. Anchor plate bolt
53. Nut
54. Friction disc
55. Friction plate
56. Mudguard clip
57. Speedometer cable clip
58. Horn grille
59. Bolt
60. Washer
61. Nut

and pump ⅙ pint (100 c.c.) of oil (*see* page 41) into each fork leg by means of a pressure can or gun.

Re-filling Model TR5 Forks. To re-fill the forks on the TR5, unscrew the two large cap nuts, securing the stanchions to the fork head lug and pour in the oil past the springs.

Under normal conditions the time between fork overhauls is estimated

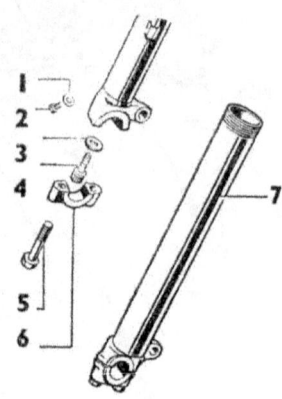

FIG. 34. MODIFICATION TO TELESCOPIC FORK LEGS (1956–9)

The general arrangement of the front forks on 1956–9 models is almost identical to that of the 1945–55 forks shown in Fig. 33 but, as shown above, the base of each fork leg has a detachable wheel spindle cap. Another very minor alteration is the substitution of a rubber washer for the felt washer shown at 15 in Fig. 33.

1. Washer
2. Drain plug
3. Aluminium washer
4. Cone and dust cover
5. One of 4 bolts for securing 6
6. Wheel-spindle cap
7. Bottom tube cover, N.S.

to be 20,000 miles. This job should be carried out by a Triumph Dealer or by the Triumph Service Department.

The fork springs have a colour identification. For solo purposes, Red: for sidecar purposes, Blue.

Adjusting the Steering Head Races. Check for play every 5,000 miles. When adjusting the steering head bearing it is necessary to support the machine on the rear or central stand and also on a box placed underneath the crankcase, so as to relieve the races of all external influence. To test the play in the steering head, slacken off the steering damper, and stand at the near-side of the motor-cycle. Rest the fingers of the right hand on the top steering-head race dust cover and with the left hand raise and lower the nose of the front mudguard (*see* Fig. 35). Any slackness calls for an immediate adjustment. It is assumed, of course, that there is no slackness in the front mudguard. If there is, stand in front of the machine and rock the front fork legs fore and aft while watching for play and feeling for play in the steering head races. Watch the lower part of the fork crown; any movement in the races will be noticeable at once. If play is present, adjust the races in the following way.

TOP LUG CLIP BOLTS. Slacken off the nut.

CROWN AND STEM NUT. The nut hexagon can be got at with a spanner if the fork is swung to the left or right. The spanner should be turned

FIG. 35. TESTING THE ADJUSTMENT OF THE STEERING HEAD RACES

clockwise to take up play, but only two-finger pressure should be applied; then ease off the pressure anti-clockwise and test.

On models 3TA and 5TA the nut on the fork sleeve stem can be turned by applying a tommy-bar instead of a spanner to the nut.

TESTING. If the adjustment is correct, the fork should move to the full lock position in both directions under its own weight. Slacken off the adjuster nut a little if the movement is sluggish, and test again. Then check the steering when riding.

WHEELS, BRAKES, TYRES

The Front Wheel (1937–39 Models). The removal of the front wheel is a straightforward operation. If it is necessary to dismantle the bearings, proceed as follows: remove the adjusting and locknuts from the near-side end of the axle and push out. The nut at the right-hand end should not be disturbed, unless it is essential to do so for some special reason. The inner spools and the roller cages can be taken clear of the outer rings. These outer rings, which are a press fit in the hub tube, may be driven out by inserting a rod of soft metal from the reverse side abutting against the inner edge of the race; they can be returned in the same way—by pressing them evenly into the housing.

The Front Wheel—1945–59 Models. The front wheel as fitted requires little in the way of maintenance beyond re-packing the hub with grease every 10,000 miles. Ball-bearing type wheel bearings, as fitted, require no adjustment. The rim is 19 in. in diameter (WM 2–19), fitted with a 3·25 × 19 in. tyre. The hub consists of two parts—the hub itself and the brake drum. An interesting point to note is that the spokes have specially angled heads, these making for sturdy wheel construction. Many of the recent models have full-width light alloy hubs.

Removing the Front Wheel (1945–55 Models). The split-pin should be removed from the pivot-pin, which connects the brake operating lever and the cable, when the pivot-pin can be withdrawn.

Remove the bolt connecting the anchor plate to the fork leg after unscrewing the nut; remove the nut from the spindles, lower the front stand by loosening the retaining nut at the rear of the mudguard and pivot the stand downwards; then slacken the spindle pinch-bolt on the left-hand fork and drive the spindle out when the wheel can be withdrawn, taking care not to damage the spindle threads.

Fitting the Front Wheel (1945–55 Models). If the front wheel is not fitted carefully, the efficient working of the front fork will be affected. Follow these instructions and the split left-hand cover tube lug, which houses the pinch-bolt, will align itself correctly.

See that the spindle is a good push fit in the split left-hand cover tube lug; if too tight, clean out the lug removing any burrs or enamel, but if this is not effective, open up the split lug gap. This is essential to ensure that the left-hand fork leg aligns itself on the spindle sleeve.

Place the wheel between the fork legs and secure in position by passing the spindle through the split lug into the wheel and through the other lug. The anchor plate should then be positioned and the mudguard bridge support clip secured with the anchor bolt. Fit the spindle nut and plain washer and tighten, but do not tighten the pinch-bolt on the opposite leg for the time being.

GENERAL MAINTENANCE: THE MOTOR-CYCLE 73

Fit the brake cable adjuster to the abutment on the anchor plate and assemble the pivot bolt to the cable fork and brake lever arm, then push a split-pin through the pivot bolt and bend the ends over to secure it. Swing the stand back into position and tighten the securing nut, check that the spindle pinch-bolt is loose and that the left-hand fork leg can slide on the spindle sleeve. Sit on the machine and, applying the front brake, work the fork up and down half a dozen times; this positions the

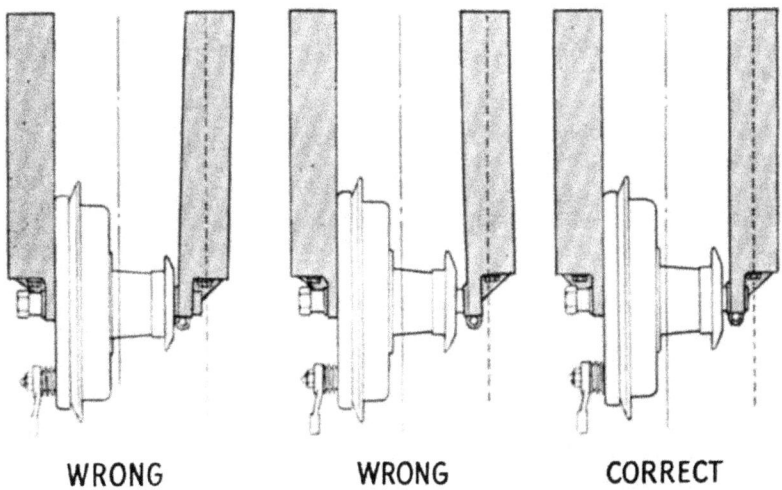

FIG. 36. CORRECT ALIGNMENT OF FRONT WHEEL IN 1945-55 FORKS
Applicable to rigid frame models.

fork leg on the spindle and prevents any binding between the stanchions and the cover tubes.

Finally, tighten up the spindle pinch-bolt.

Removing the Front Wheel (1956-9 Models). Withdraw the split pin and pivot pin from the lower end of the brake cable. On the earlier models TR6, T100 and T110 unscrew the nut and remove the bolt which secures the anchor plate to the fork leg. Remove the two bolts which secure each wheel-spindle cap (6, Fig. 34) to the corresponding bottom-tube cover on the fork leg. Slacken the retaining nut at the rear of the mudguard and swing the front stand forward. Then withdraw the front wheel from the telescopic forks.

Fitting the Front Wheel (1956-9 Models). Position the front wheel in the telescopic forks and swing the front stand backwards. If handy, add a small weight in front of the parcel grid on the petrol tank to ensure that the fork legs rest on the wheel spindle. Hold the wheel-spindle caps (6, Fig. 34) in position and screw the cap-securing bolts a few turns into the front fork bottom-tube covers (7, Fig. 32). Note that the wheel spindle is recessed at the bolt positions and it may prove necessary to move the front wheel slightly from side to side before it is possible to insert the four cap-securing bolts. At this stage do not fully tighten the four bolts.

On all models with full-width light alloy hubs see that the anchor peg on the off-side fork leg engages with the channel on the brake anchor plate. On the earlier TR6, T100 and T110 models insert the brake anchor bolt and tighten it securely.

Tighten the four spindle cap-securing bolts (5, Fig. 34) evenly; keep the space between each cap and fork leg equal in front of and behind the wheel spindle. Refit the front brake cable to the abutment and insert the pivot pin and split pin. Check that the handlebar adjustment for the front brake is correct (*see* page 78). With the front stand in its normal position tighten the securing nut.

Centralizing Brake Shoes. On *all* models loosen the nut on the front brake fulcrum pin and apply strong pressure with the handlebar lever. Keep this pressure on the lever while tightening the fulcrum pin nut. The two brake shoes should then be properly synchronized.

The Rear Wheel (Rigid Frame Models). The Triumph rear wheel has taper-roller bearings and requires occasional adjustment. Any slackness in the bearings can be felt when the motor-cycle is raised on the rear stand. Check for slackness every 2,000–3,000 miles. The lateral movement should be hardly noticeable. The bearings are held in adjustment by locknuts and the lateral movement should be checked after the locknuts have been tightened. The hubs are packed with grease; repacking is only necessary every 10,000 miles. The rim is 19 in. in diameter (WM 2–19) and the tyre is a 3·50 × 19 in. As with the front wheel the spokes are of four different head shapes; note this carefully when making replacements. The brakes are 7 in. (17·78 cm) internally expanding and are located on a mild steel anchor-plate which has a strong external peg locating in a channel in the frame to withstand the braking torque.

Removing the Rear Wheel (Rigid Frame Models). The procedure is as follows. Remove the mudguard on all models with the exception of model TR5. Disconnect the rear light leads beneath the saddle, unscrew the nuts connecting the mudguard to the frame, and remove the mudguard. Take the rear chain off the rear sprocket after removing the spring link, but first engage a gear in order to prevent the gearbox sprocket from rotating and allowing the chain to fall off; remove the brake rod from the lever arm; and slacken the two rear-spindle nuts and withdraw the wheel.

GENERAL MAINTENANCE: THE MOTOR-CYCLE 75

Fitting the Rear Wheel (Rigid Frame Models). Lift the rear wheel into the frame with the brake drum on the left-hand side. Engage the anchor plate lug "A" into "B" on the inside of the left-hand fork lug (*see* Fig. 37). Push the wheel up to the chain adjuster screws and tighten the spindle nuts.

When the wheel is in the frame, test the wheel bearings for adjustment. If further adjustment be necessary, it should be made before final assembly, but remember that the right-hand spindle nut should be loosened before any adjustment is attempted.

At this stage pull the brake lever arm back, thread the brake rod through the pivot roller in the lever arm and screw on the brake adjusting thumbnut until the wheel turns freely without the brakes binding. If it has been

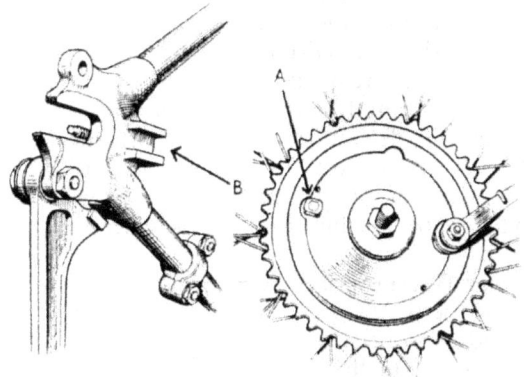

FIG. 37. STUD *A* ON REAR BRAKE ANCHOR PLATE WHICH MUST BE LOCATED IN REAR FORK CHANNEL *B*

necessary to fit new brake linings, the brakes should be bedded in before correct adjustment is possible. This ensures the wheel running freely.

Connect up the chain round the sprocket and replace the spring link so that the closed end is facing the direction of travel.

Return the mudguard to the frame and connect the tail lamp leads under the saddle. Check the working of the stop light and make final adjustment to the brakes after testing on the road.

The Rear Wheel (Spring Frame Models). The Triumph rear wheel is mounted on journal ball bearings and these bearings need no adjustment. Only after a very big mileage is it necessary to check for bearing slackness. Slackness can be easily checked by placing the motor-cycle on its central stand and testing for lateral movement of the rear wheel. If the bearings are in good shape a negligible amount of lateral movement should be detected. Note that other details concerning the rear wheel are the same as for the wheel on rigid frame models (*see* page 74).

Removing the Rear Wheel (Spring Frame Models). On "swinging arm" models the following procedure should be used. First engage a gear to prevent the secondary chain rotating on the gearbox sprocket, and falling off when the chain spring-link is removed. Remove the spring link and withdraw the secondary chain from the sprocket. Disconnect the rear brake torque stay by removing the rear nut and loosening the front nut and bolt. Unscrew the brake adjuster nut and remove the brake rod from the lever arm. On models 3TA and 5TA disconnect the speedometer cable from the gearbox.

Now unscrew the two rear-wheel spindle nuts and remove them from the spindle. Pull the rear wheel back in the frame a short distance and disconnect the chain adjusters from the rear wheel spindle. On all 1956-9 models after disconnecting the chain adjusters loosen the nut near the bottom of the near-side rear Girling suspension unit and swing the chain guard upward prior to removing the rear wheel. Now remove the rear wheel from the spring frame as shown in Fig. 38. Note that if you have a prop stand fitted, you should lower it to steady the motor-cycle during wheel removal. Some tilting of the machine is necessary. Stand on the near-side of the motor-cycle and tilt it on to the left leg of the central stand. Reach across the machine and pull the wheel clear of the fork ends.

Fitting the Rear Wheel (Spring Frame Models). Tilt the machine to the left and position the wheel between the swinging fork, but see that the anchor plate stud is properly located in the brake torque-stay hole. Reposition the brake rod to the brake lever; fit the chain adjusters to the spindle and position the end plates; fit the chain to the sprocket and replace the connecting link, check the tension of the chain and adjust as necessary.

Screw the nuts on to the spindle and tighten them; fit the rear nut of the brake torque-stay and tighten both nuts: on models 3TA and 5TA swing the chain guard downwards and engage it with the bolt and tighten firmly the securing nut. Finally, spin the wheel and note the operation of the brake pedal and adjust as required. On models 3TA and 5TA fit the speedometer cable to the gearbox so that the squared end engages fully and then tighten the cable nut.

The Rear Wheel (Quickly Detachable). This wheel is fitted to the swinging-fork or -arm frame only. It is mounted on three bearings—two roller bearings in the hub and a journal ball bearing in the brake drum centre. The wheel can be taken out quickly, because the method of construction adopted is that of splining the hub into the brake drum, so there is no need to remove the secondary chain or to disconnect the rear brake. All other details are as for the rigid-frame rear wheel (*see* page 74).

Removing the Q.D. Rear Wheel. Insert a suitable tommy spanner bar through the hexagon-shaped spindle end (right-hand side) or use a spanner and unscrew until the spindle can be withdrawn. Then remove the distance piece from between the right-hand fork and the wheel.

Ease the wheel to the right-hand side until the hub splines are clear of the brake drum splines; tilt the machine to the left (pull out the prop stand if one be fitted and use as a steady) when the wheel can be removed from the right-hand side (*see* Fig. 38).

Fitting the Q.D. Wheel to the Frame and Brake Drum. First fit a new rubber seal over the hub splines then, with the machine tilted over as when dismantling, enter the wheel between the forks, right the machine and locate the hub splines into the brake drum splines. Next, fit the collar with the cone-shaped end towards the hexagon to the spindle, then the chain adjuster with the stud inwards, then the distance piece between the fork and wheel and insert the spindle through the wheel and screw it into the hub sleeve. Fit the chain adjuster end-plate to the right-hand adjuster stud and fork end and secure with the nut. Lastly, check the chain and brake adjustments and the wheel alignment. When correct, tighten the left-hand wheel nut and then place a bar or spanner to the spindle hexagon and turn until the spindle is tight. Check the brake torque-stay nuts for tightness.

FIG. 38. REMOVING WHEEL FROM SPRING FRAME

The Mk. 2 Spring Wheel (Earlier Models). This wheel operates for long periods without maintenance. No provision is made for greasing, for instance, as before assembly the bearings and other working surfaces are loaded with sufficient grease for 20,000 miles. Check the wheel bearings for play every 5,000 miles.

When this wheel requires attention—dismantling and assembling—special equipment is needed and owners are strongly advised to return the wheel to their dealer or direct to the Triumph Service Department for rectification.

In view of the above, the only details described are the removal of the wheel from the frame and refitting the wheel to the frame.

Removing Spring Wheel (Earlier Models). To remove the wheel from the frame, first disconnect the rear light leads under the saddle, then remove the bolts connecting the rear part of the mudguard to the frame and lift the rear part away (*see* Fig. 39). There is no need to disturb the mudguard of model TR5 when removing the wheel. Take out the rear chain spring-link and remove the chain from the sprocket, engaging a gear to prevent

FIG. 39. REAR PART OF MUDGUARD REMOVED TO FACILITATE REMOVAL OF SPRING WHEEL (MK. 2)

Applicable to earlier type models.

the chain rolling off the sprocket. Unscrew the adjuster and depress the brake pedal to clear the brake rod from the brake lever arm, then unscrew the two locknuts at the top of the anchor plate pivot and remove the pivot bolt, and finally remove the two spindle nuts and distance collars and withdraw the wheel from the frame.

Adjusting Both Brakes. The wheels must be raised off the ground, before making any adjustment, by placing the machine on its stand or stands as the case may be.

To adjust the brake shoes closer to the brake drum, in the case of the front brake, turn the knurled thumb-nut (*A*, Fig. 40) in a *clockwise* direction. The brakes should be set so that when fully applied the lever is just clear of the handlebar. If this be done, the rider is able to exert the

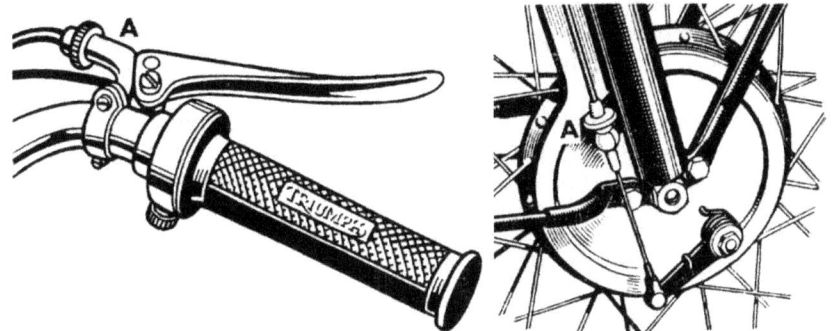

Fig. 40. The Two Types of Front Brake Adjustment

The adjustment is shown at *A*. On the left is the handlebar adjustment on all 1956-9 models. On the right is the adjustment on 1945-55 and earlier models.

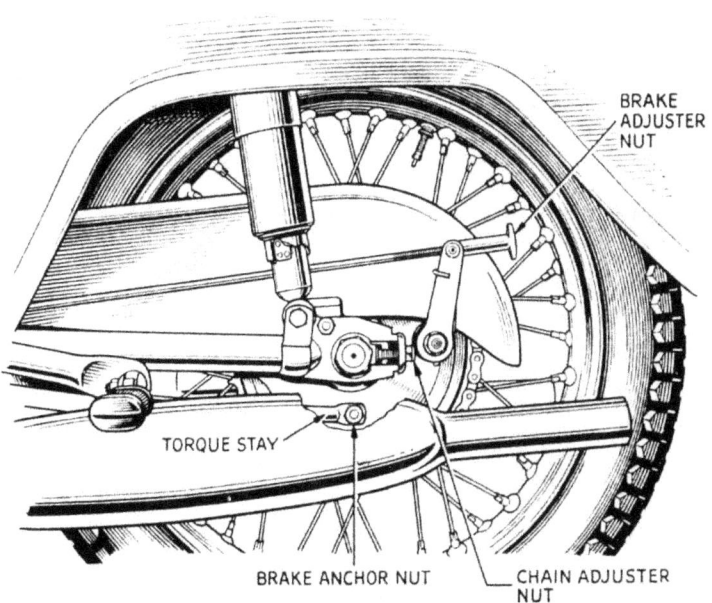

Fig. 41. The Rear Brake and Secondary Chain Adjustment on 1956-9 Models

The illustration shows the details on a model 3TA and 5TA, but the adjustments are similar on all 1956-9 machines. On earlier rigid frame models the brake adjustment is the same, but the secondary chain has a different adjustment (*see* Fig. 42).

maximum amount of grip on the lever. Spin the wheel after making this adjustment to ensure that the brake shoes are not binding on the brake drum.

The adjustment of the rear brake is made by turning the knurled thumb-nut (*A*, Fig. 40) at the rear end of the brake operating rod in a *clockwise* direction. Spin the wheel after adjusting to make certain that the brake is not binding. On the rigid-frame models an adjustment can be made to the brake pedal position but, after making an alteration, re-adjust the brake. Brake adjustment is normally required every 1,000 miles.

The Tyres. The tyres must be maintained at the correct inflation pressure if they are to provide safe and comfortable riding, a long life and immunity from trouble. The pressure should be checked every week, a reliable pressure gauge being used for the purpose. Suitable pressure gauges are the Holdtite, the Dunlop pencil-type No. 6, the Schroder 7750, and the Romac.

Where a pillion passenger is carried it is usually advisable to increase the pressure of the rear tyre by 4–5 lb per sq in. Generally speaking, it is advisable to run the rear tyre at a moderate pressure, consistent with good steering. If the tyre is too soft the machine will tend to wander, and if too hard, riding will be uncomfortable and the rear wheel will tend to bounce. The exact tyre pressures used depend upon the rider's weight and the type of machine, and are to some extent a matter for individual experiment.

RECOMMENDED DUNLOP TYRE PRESSURES (1945–59 SOLO MODELS)

Triumph Solo Models ("Swinging Arm")		Tyre Size	Inflation (lb per sq in.)
5T, 6T, T110 and T120	Front	3·25 × 19	18
	Rear	3·50 × 19	19
T100	Front	3·25 × 19	17
	Rear	3·50 × 19	19
TR5 and TR6	Front	3·00 × 20	21
	Front	3·25 × 19	18
	Rear	4·00 × 18	16
3TA and 5TA	Front	3·25 × 17	20
	Rear	3·25 × 17	22
	Rear	3·50 × 17	20

The correct average tyre inflation pressures for 1945–59 Triumph twin-cylinder models are tabulated above. These pressures apply to solo models and are based on the rider's weight being not more than 170 lb. Add 1 lb per sq in. for every 28 lb increase in weight above 170 lb, in the

GENERAL MAINTENANCE: THE MOTOR-CYCLE 81

case of the front tyre. Where the rear tyre is concerned, add 1 lb per sq in. for every 14 lb increase in weight above 170 lb. Where an extra load is carried in the form of a pillion passenger or luggage, determine the actual load on each tyre (on a weighbridge at a railway station or large transport depot) and then use the minimum tyre pressures for specific loads recommended in the accompanying Dunlop table.

MINIMUM TYRE PRESSURES FOR SPECIFIC LOADS

Nominal Tyre Section (in)	Inflation Pressures (lb per sq in.)					
	16	18	20	24	28	32
	Load per Tyre (lb)					
2·375	120	140	160	185	210	240
2·50	120	140	160	185	210	240
2·75	140	160	180	210	250	280
3·00	160	180	200	240	300	350
3·25	200	240	280	350	400	440
3·50	280	320	350	400	450	500
4·00	360	400	430	500	—	—

(*By courtesy of The Dunlop Rubber Co., Ltd.*)

The tyres should be examined regularly, particularly after riding over roads which have been tarred and gritted, and any sharp pieces of stone or flint should be removed with a pen-knife. If allowed to remain, no immediate danger may be caused, but ultimately they will work right through the cover and puncture the tube.

Punctured Rear Tyre (Rigid Frame Models). Should it be necessary to mend a puncture, the removal of the rear wheel is not necessary. As may be seen in Fig. 39, a large circumference of the rear wheel is accessible by removing the rear part of the mudguard. On all spring frame models the rear wheel must be removed to effect a tyre repair.

CHAIN MAINTENANCE

Badly adjusted chains are a frequent cause of harsh running and excessive wear. It is therefore of great importance to see that the primary and secondary chains are correctly adjusted (check tension every 1,000 miles) and properly lubricated. Lubrication has already been dealt with in Chapter III. On *rigid frame* models the correct tension of the primary and secondary chains is ½ in. and ¾ in. respectively. On (1945–59) "*swinging arm*" *spring frame* models the correct primary chain tension is ½ in. The correct secondary chain tension is ¾ in. with the machine off its stand or 1¼ in. *with the machine on its stand.* Chain "tension" means the total up and down chain deflection possible with the fingers, near the chain centre vertically, with the chain in its tightest position.

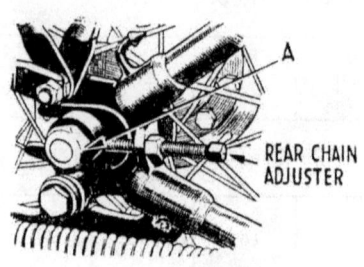

Fig. 42. Showing Rear Chain Adjuster (1937–9)

Primary Chain Adjustment (1937–9 Models). On 1937–9 models, access to the gearbox clamping nut is best obtained by removing the off-side footrest, and pushing the spindle out of the way. It is then possible to use a spanner on the nut satisfactorily. It should be particularly noted that failure to slacken the clamping nut when making chain tension adjustment will result in a fractured gearbox casing. Access to the gearbox trunnion bolt is obtained from beneath the machine, between the mudguard and gearbox.

When adjusting the secondary chain great care should be exercised not to interfere with the alignment; it is essential to adjust each side of the axle equally. This is, however, quite a simple operation. All that is necessary is to slacken the outside axle nuts (*A*, Fig. 42) and the locknuts on the adjusters, rotate the latter in a clockwise direction to tighten, moving each one the same number of turns, finally securing all the nuts. Adjusting the tension of the rear chain affects the adjustment of the brake (*see* page 80).

Primary Chain Adjustment (Rigid Frame Models, 1945 Onwards). The gearbox pivot bolt locates the gearbox to the lower frame and must be loosened before making an adjustment.

To gain access to the nut on the gearbox clamp bolt, remove the right-hand footrest and push the spindle out of the way; then a spanner can be applied to the nut.

The chain adjuster is located above the gearbox (*see* Fig. 43) and to slacken the chain, turn the adjuster anti-clockwise; turn clockwise to tighten. When tightening the chain always pull the gearbox back after adjusting and test the chain tension again. This is necessary because the loading on the rear chain pulls the gearbox towards the rear so the tension of the chain is altered.

Finally, re-tighten the clamping nut and pivot bolt and make certain they are secure.

Secondary Chain Adjustment (Rigid Frame Models, 1945 Onwards). First slacken off both wheel nuts. The adjusters are placed in the rear

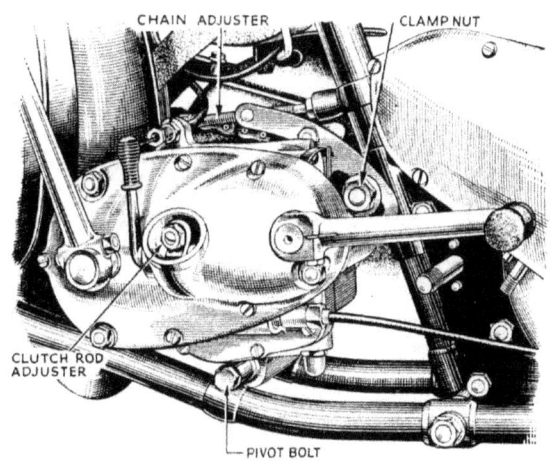

Fig. 43. Showing Primary Chain and Other Adjustment Points (1945 and Later Rigid Frame Models)

frame fork ends; to tighten the chain slacken-off the adjuster locknuts and tighten the adjuster (clockwise). Great care must be taken not to interfere with the alignment of the rear wheel, so it is important to see that both adjusters are turned an equal number of times. To slacken the chain, reverse the order. Tighten the adjuster locknuts and spindle nuts, then check the adjustment of the brake.

Primary Chain Adjustment (Swinging-arm Models). No adjustment is necessary on models 3TA, 5TA. On other machines the gearbox pivot bolt secures the gearbox to the lower frame and must be slackened before adjusting the primary chain. Slacken the securing nut of the gearbox clamping bolt (*see* Fig. 44) which positions the adjuster. To tighten the primary chain, slacken off the front locknut a few turns and tighten up the rear locknut until the tension is correct; to slacken the chain, reverse the order. Lastly, re-tighten the clamp nut, locknuts and pivot bolt and see they are absolutely secure.

Secondary Chain Adjustment (Swinging-arm Models). This adjustment can be carried out with the machine off the stand, ¾ in. vertical play, or on the stand, 1¼ in. vertical play.

Slacken off both wheel nuts and the brake anchor nut (models 3TA, 5TA). The adjusters are on the wheel spindle and the swinging-fork end lugs (*see* Fig. 41). To tighten the secondary chain, turn the adjuster nuts clockwise *an equal number of times* until the correct tension is secured; to slacken, reverse the order and push the wheel forward against the adjuster

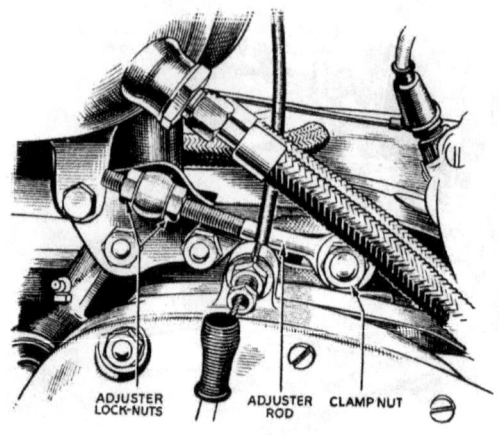

Fig. 44. Primary Chain Adjustment on 1945–59 "Swinging Arm" Models

Applies to all except models 3TA and 5TA whose primary chains (duplex) need no adjustment.

end plates. Finally, tighten the adjuster locknuts and wheel spindle nuts (also brake anchor nut on 3TA, 5TA); then check the brake adjustment and wheel alignment (*see* page 78).

Cleaning Chains. The owner should, of course, see that both chains are properly lubricated but, in addition, the secondary chain should be removed at intervals and cleaned thoroughly and re-greased.

To clean and re-grease the secondary chain may take a little time, but it is well worth while doing the job properly. Take off this chain and brush off all external dirt with a wire brush. To remove dirt and old grease from the joints, soak the chain in a paraffin bath and move it about until it is thoroughly clean, then rinse it in clean paraffin and hang it up to drain and dry. After drying, re-lubricate it by immersing it in a bath of grease which has been melted over a pan of boiling water and allow it to remain for five to ten minutes, and during this period it should be moved about freely so that the grease penetrates into the bearings. When the grease has cooled to its normal state take the chain out of the bath, wipe off all surplus grease and replace the chain on the machine. Fitting the spring clip fastener on the connecting link is simple, provided the rider remembers

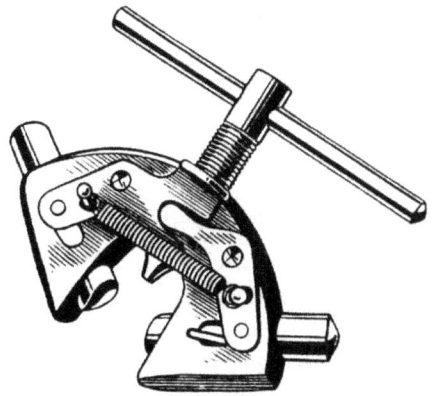

FIG. 45 (A). RIVET EXTRACTOR WITH JAWS OPEN

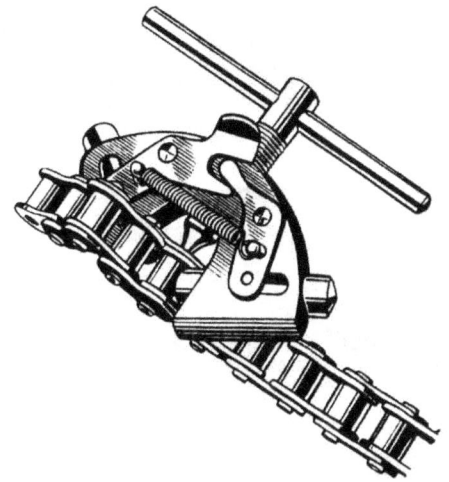

FIG. 45 (B). RIVET EXTRACTOR IN POSITION

this—the fastener is like a fish in shape—a fish swims nose first and the fastener must be fitted so that the nose (the closed end) always proceeds in the forward direction when the motor-cycle is running.

The owner is advised to clean and re-grease the secondary chain at the beginning of the winter, halfway through the winter and at the beginning of the summer.

86   THE BOOK OF THE TRIUMPH TWINS

Chain Alterations and Repairs. In the event of it being necessary to repair, lengthen or shorten a chain, a rivet extractor and a few spare parts will be required. The rivet extractor (*see* Fig. 45A and B) is suitable for chains up to ¾ in. pitch, whether they are on or off the wheels.

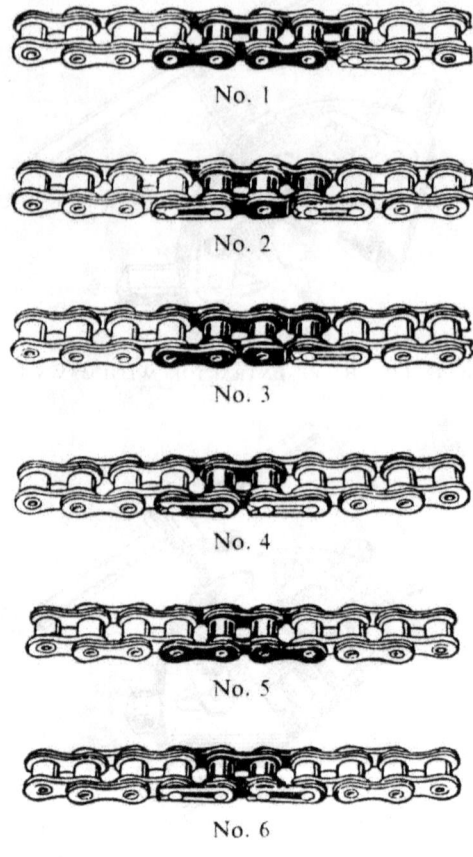

FIG. 46. AVAILABLE CHAIN LINKS

To shorten a chain containing an even number of pitches, remove the dark parts shown in No. 1, Fig. 46, and replace by a cranked double-link and single-connecting link, No. 2.

To shorten a chain containing an odd number of pitches, remove the dark parts shown in No. 3, and replace by a single connecting link and inner link, No. 4.

To repair a chain with a broken roller or inside link, remove the dark

GENERAL MAINTENANCE: THE MOTOR-CYCLE   87

parts in No. 5, and replace by two single connecting links and one inner link, No. 6.

FRAME AND SIDECAR HINTS

The "Swinging-arm" Frame. The swinging fork is pivoted to the main frame by a ground hollow spindle. Two phosphor-bronze bushes are

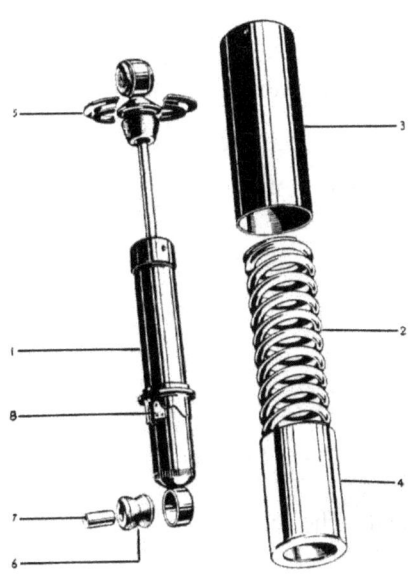

FIG. 47. GIRLING HYDRAULIC DAMPER UNIT (1945–55)
The 1956–9 unit is considerably altered.

1. Damper unit
2. Suspension spring
3. Upper dirt-shield
4. Lower dirt-shield
5. Spring retainer
6. Rubber bearing bush
7. Bearing bush sleeve
8. Cam spring abutment

pressed into the fork bridge lug to provide a bearing surface on which the fork swings. The spindle is a light drive fit into the frame lug and a working fit in the fork bushes. To retain the spindle in position, a rod is passed through the hollow in the spindle and at each end a retainer cap is made captive by nuts screwed on the rod ends. A spacing washer is fitted between the bridge lug and the frame lug on the right-hand side, so as to obtain the clearance which should on 1945–55 models be between 0·0005 in.–0·0065 in. (0·013–0·16 mm). On 1956–9 models the clearance (new) is up to 0·005 in. (0·125 mm). *Shims are available to take up excessive clearance.* A grease nipple is fitted to the frame to provide access for grease to the bearing by means of a grease gun. Apply the grease gun every 1,500 miles.

The life of the bearing bushes is approximately 20,000 miles under average running conditions. To replace the bushes is an operation of a major type and, therefore, the owner is advised to put the work in the hands of a Triumph Dealer.

Girling Suspension Damper Units. These units are completely self-contained and are known under the type number S/MDA/4/4 or (1956-9) SB4.

Maintenance is negligible during the normal life of the unit. The owner will experience no difficulty in changing such parts as the main spring and rubber bushes, but if the hydraulic unit be suspected, he should not

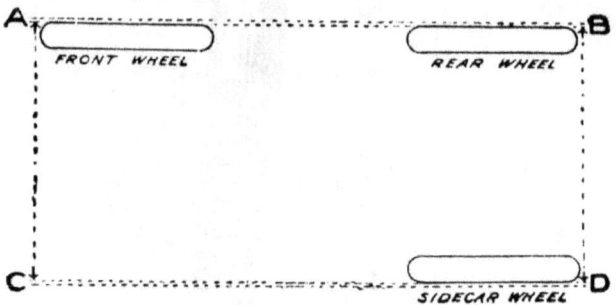

FIG. 48. SIDECAR ALIGNMENT

attempt to dismantle it. The complete units should be returned to a Lucas Girling Depot, or to the manufacturers, who can supply a service unit or rectify the fault.

Should you have additional weight on the rear of your Triumph, such as a heavy pillion passenger or pannier equipment with luggage, the swinging fork member will position itself above the horizontal. The effect of this is to reduce the springing potential. To remedy this condition, you should increase the poundage in each Girling suspension damper unit by turning the spring abutment cam (*see* Fig. 49) with the *C* spanner supplied for this purpose in the tool-kit. The adjustment is best made with the machine on its central stand.

The Sidecar. With straight edges placed alongside the machine, sidecar wheels, the lateral adjustment should provide that the dimension immediately ahead of the front wheel, line *A—C*, is $\frac{1}{2}$ in. less than that behind the rear wheels, line *B—D*, as shown in Fig. 48. The telescopic arms should be adjusted so that the machine leans slightly out of the vertical to the off side. Always follow the sidecar maker's instructions.

To maintain the sidecar in good running order the spring bearing nipples should be greased frequently, while periodically the leaves should be separated and a little grease inserted. The wheel should be tested for

GENERAL MAINTENANCE: THE MOTOR-CYCLE

play. Play can be taken up by removing the outer cap and the split-pin, and then easing the castellated nut back a few turns and rotating the adjusting cone, as necessary.

Attaching a Sidecar. Note that stronger telescopic front-fork springs are required for a sidecar outfit than for a solo model. If you attach a sidecar to a Triumph bought for solo use, take the motor-cycle to a

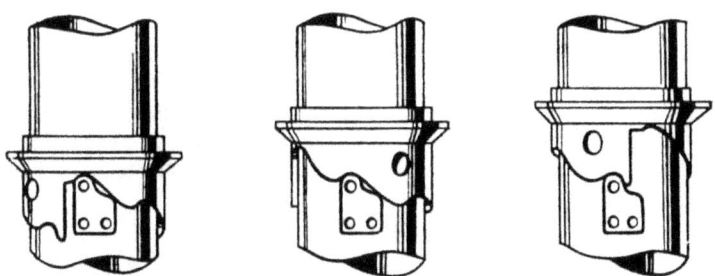

FIG. 49. GIRLING SUSPENSION DAMPER UNIT ADJUSTMENT

On the left is shown the first position for a light load, in the centre the second position for a medium load, and on the right the third position for a heavy load.

Triumph dealer and get him to fit heavy-duty springs to the telescopic front-forks. Do not attempt to fit the springs yourself.

THE GEARBOX AND CLUTCH

The Gearbox (1945–59 Models). The gearbox is of Triumph design and manufacture. It has four speeds and is very strongly made. Very little attention is normally required, but it is essential to keep the gearbox properly lubricated (*see* page 33). Check that its clamping-bolt nuts are tight, at convenient periods. Should any serious gearbox trouble develop it is best to take the machine or gearbox to a Triumph dealer who undertakes repairs. Provided that the machine is handled properly, however, gearbox trouble rarely develops. Special gears are obtainable for those who wish to indulge in racing, but racing requirements are beyond the scope of this handbook which deals with touring models.

Clutch Adjustment (All 1945–59 Models Except 3TA and 5TA). There should always be a free movement in the clutch cable of about $\frac{1}{8}$ in. Without this free movement the clutch is liable to slip, and rapid wear of the plate inserts will inevitably occur.

Where an adjustment is necessary, screw in the adjuster inside the gearbox filler cap (*see* Fig. 43) until the lever leans out about 15 degrees. Then adjust the cable at the lug on top of the gearbox to give the required $\frac{1}{8}$ in. free movement of the clutch cable.

Clutch Adjustment (Models 3TA and 5TA). Loosen the knurled finger adjustment at the handlebar lever (*see* Fig. 1). Then loosen the locknut in the centre of the clutch pressure plate and screw in the adjuster until the pressure plate just starts to lift. Afterwards screw it back *one-half turn*. If the gear change pedal is stiff, slacken the adjuster a little more until it becomes free. Now tighten the locknut. Finally turn the knurled finger-adjustment until there is not less than $\frac{1}{8}$ in. free movement in the clutch cable.

Clutch Adjustment (1937–9 Models). To obtain the required free cable movement of $\frac{1}{8}$ in. a locknut and screw are provided at the abutment on the gearbox inner cover. There is also a screw and locknut beneath the gearbox filler cap. Always maintain a slight amount of play between the clutch arm and the push-rod which operates the clutch plates.

Clutch and Shock-absorber Unit (1945–59 Models). The clutch on all 1945–59 models is of the multi-plate, cork type incorporating a transmission shock-absorber. The pressure on the plates is exerted by four equally disposed springs, which can be adjusted by screwing in or out the four slotted nuts which secure them. It is important to see that the oil level in the chain case is maintained correct as the clutch is designed to operate in oil; otherwise the cork inserts may burn and disintegrate under heavy loading. Only the recommended grade of oil should be used, because if a heavier one be used, the clutch plates will not separate properly when disengaged and this causes difficult and noisy gear-selection when the foot-change pedal is used. Always operate the kickstarter a few times with the clutch withdrawn before starting the engine. This makes certain that the plates separate freely when a gear selection is made.

The shock-absorber unit is strongly constructed and is designed to give many thousands of miles of service. It operates as follows. The drive is transmitted through the clutch plates in the normal way, then through the drive rubbers to the four-armed spider which is keyed to the clutch shaft and this is also keyed to the gearbox mainshaft. The spider is free to oscillate inside the clutch centre, but it is restrained by eight rubber pads, two on either side of each arm. The four larger pads are the drive rubbers, the smaller the rebound. The drive and rebound rubbers level out all the engine speed variations at low speeds and this provides an extremely smooth and pleasant torque, while transmission wear is reduced due to the absence of snatch.

To Remove Clutch Plates (1945–59 Clutch and Shock-absorber Unit). Remove the near-side exhaust pipe and silencer. Also remove the near-side footrest and rear brake pedal unit. Lay a drip-tray beneath the primary chaincase and remove the securing screws from the chaincase. Then withdraw the outer cover from the oilbath chaincase. Where a coil ignition model is concerned be most careful not to damage the stator windings (*see* Fig. 22).

Remove the four slotted nuts from the outside of the clutch and shock-absorber unit. The correct method of doing this is shown in Fig. 51. Unscrew the nuts by using the special key *B* which is provided in the tool kit. On the under side of each nut head is a small "pip" which contacts

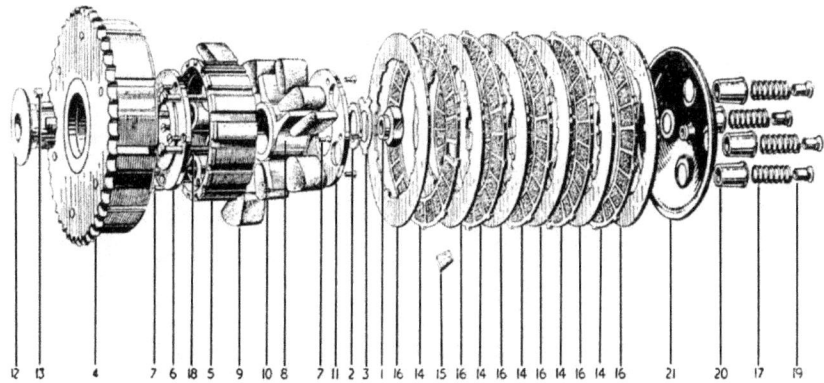

Fig. 50. Exploded View of Clutch and Shock-absorber Unit

1. Nut (clutch to mainshaft)
2. Plain washer
3. Lock washer
4. Clutch-sprocket housing
5. Clutch centre
6. Inner shock-absorber retaining plate
7. Screw
8. Shock-absorber spider
9. Rubber insert (driving)
10. Rubber insert (rebound)
11. Outer shock-absorber plate
12. Clutch hub
13. Roller (housing to hub)
14. Driving plate
15. Langite insert
16. Driven plate
17. Clutch pressure spring
18. Clutch pressure-spring pin
19. Clutch pressure-spring pin nut
20. Clutch pressure-spring cup
21. Clutch pressure-plate

the end of the spring coil. This serves as an efficient locking device and renders it impossible for the nut to turn while the clutch is in motion. To assist nut removal, insert a knife blade (*A*, Fig. 51) beneath the head of the nut so as to keep the spring away from the "pip" during the unscrewing of the nut.

Referring to Fig. 50, withdraw the four clutch pressure-springs 17 from the clutch pressure-spring cups 20. Remove the clutch pressure-plate 21 complete with the spring cups 20. Now withdraw the driving plates 14 and the driven plates 16 from the clutch-sprocket housing 4. No further dismantling is needed if only service relined clutch plates (including cork insert plates) are required to be fitted. If the shock-absorber unit shows no signs of wear, do not disturb it. Examine the rubber inserts.

Renewal of Clutch Plates. On earlier models cork inserts are fitted, but all later models have Neo-Langite friction material bonded to the plates. This friction material cannot be renewed by the owner, and service replacement plates should be obtained from a Triumph dealer. Cork inserts can be fitted by the owner, but this is not recommended. The operation calls

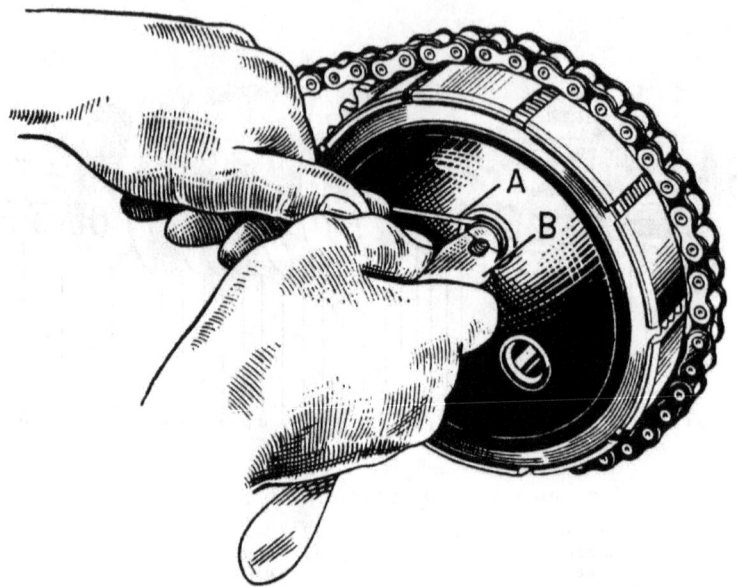

FIG. 51. HOW TO REMOVE THE FOUR NUTS FROM THE CLUTCH ASSEMBLY

for precision and special equipment to reduce the new cork inserts to the correct thickness at each side of the plate, and to ensure an even overall surface. Service replacement plates should be obtained.

Replacement plates should be fitted when there is a tendency for clutch slip to occur in spite of the clutch adjustment being correct. Metal-to-metal contact of the driving with the driven plates can be observed by ring formation, and it is not difficult to note badly worn cork inserts or bonded friction linings; the bonded linings become charred and peel away from the plates. Note that where bonded linings are fitted, the linings are not affected by petrol, oil or paraffin.

CHAPTER VI

GENERAL MAINTENANCE: THE ENGINE

This chapter deals with some important aspects of engine maintenance such as valve clearance adjustment, valve timing, ignition timing, decarbonizing, etc. For detailed information on carburettor tuning and maintenance, engine lubrication and the ignition system, *see* Chapters II to IV.

VALVE CLEARANCES

Models 5T, 6T, 3TA, 5TA and T100. These models are fitted with camshafts employing a ramp-cam form which makes it necessary to maintain a 0·010 in. (0·26 mm) clearance when *cold* between each valve rocker adjusting pin and the valve tip so as to ensure silent operation and maximum efficiency. If the clearance be appreciably less, the valve timing is affected and this results in loss of power and the chance of burnt valves.

When adjusting (cold) remove all four rocker-box inspection caps from the rocker boxes.

To position the valves, first remove the sparking plugs, then turn the engine by the kickstarter until the left exhaust valve is fully open, as this makes sure that the right exhaust valve tappet is making contact with the base of the cam, and the valve clearance at the right exhaust rocker should be set to 0·010 in. Afterwards the engine must be turned until the right exhaust valve is fully open and the valve clearance at the left exhaust rocker should be checked and adjusted. A similar sequence should be used for checking and adjusting the inlet valve clearances. All four valve clearances should be checked and adjusted every 3,000–4,000 miles. In the case of the Triumph engine a feeler gauge adjustment is not used. The following is the correct procedure for making the rocker pin adjustment.

Slacken off the rocker adjuster-pin locknut and screw down the adjuster until it just contacts the valve tip. Use the spanner shown in Figs. 52 and 53.

When the adjuster contacts the valve tip, hold the adjuster firmly with the spanner and tighten up the locknut with the other spanner, then grip the rocker adjuster between the thumb and forefinger and move the rocker sideways to test for freedom of movement and test the up-and-down movement where the clearance between the adjuster and valve tip should be just perceptible.

So that the 0·010 in. (0·26 mm) clearance may be obtained, first take note of the position of the squared end of the adjuster and with both spanners in position, slacken the locknut slightly, but do not move the adjuster. Then slacken off the adjuster one flat (*one quarter of a turn*) and, maintaining it in the new position, re-tighten the locknut. Use the same procedure for each valve clearance adjustment.

Models TR5, TR6, T110 and T120. These four models have high-lift camshafts and no silencing ramps are included in the cam form. The valve clearances required are therefore different from those required for the five models just dealt with. The correct inlet and exhaust valve clearances are

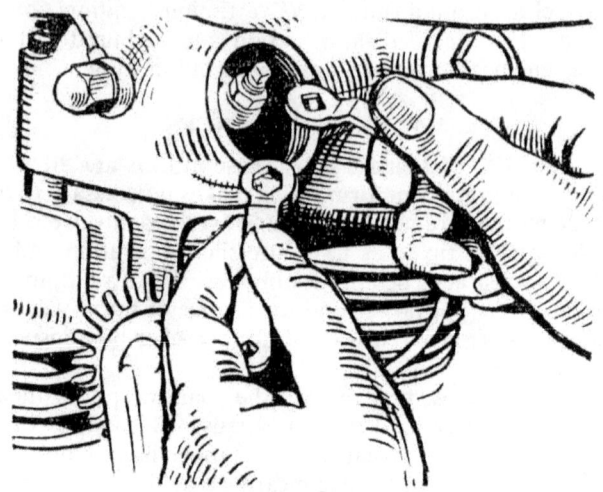

FIG. 52. VALVE CLEARANCE ADJUSTMENT ON MODELS 5T, 6T, TR5, TR6, T100, T110 AND T120

0·002 in. (0·05 mm) and 0·004 in. (0·10 mm) respectively. The adjustment must always be made *with the engine cold*. To make an adjustment, use the following procedure.

First remove all four caps from the rocker boxes. Also remove both sparking plugs from the cylinder heads. With the kick-starter rotate the engine slowly until the *left* exhaust valve is fully open. The right tappet is now resting on the base of the cam, and the valve clearance at the *right* exhaust rocker should be set to 0·004 in. Then turn the engine until the right exhaust valve is wide open and proceed to adjust the valve clearance at the left exhaust rocker. A similar sequence must be used to set the inlet valve clearances at 0·002 in. For actual rocker pin adjustment, use the two tools shown in Fig. 53. These are supplied in the tool kit.

Loosen the locknut on the rocker adjuster-pin and screw *down* the adjuster pin until it just makes contact with the tip of the valve stem. Then hold the adjuster pin firmly with the spanner and tighten up the locknut with the other spanner. Now grip the rocker and adjuster-pin between the forefinger and thumb and move the rocker sideways to test for freedom of movement. Next test the up-and-down movement. The valve clearance should be just perceptible.

The exhaust valve clearance having been made just perceptible as described in the previous paragraph, to obtain the required 0·004 in. clearance,

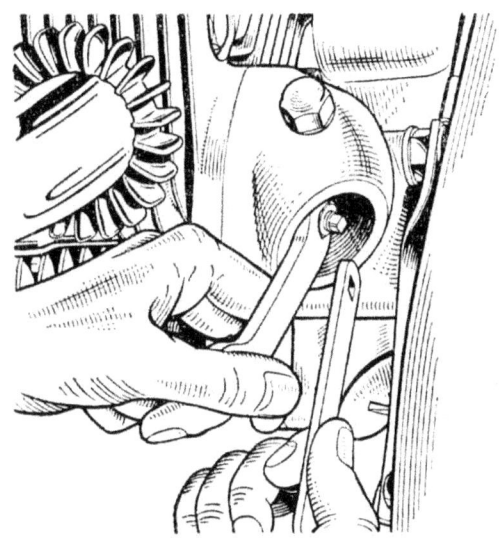

FIG. 53. VALVE CLEARANCE ADJUSTMENT ON MODELS 3TA AND 5TA

slacken back the adjuster pin half a flat (*one-eighth of a turn*). This may be slightly in excess of the valve clearance figure recommended, but the error is on the right side. For the inlet valve clearance, slightly slacken off the adjuster pin so that when the rocker adjuster-pin is gripped between the thumb and forefinger and moved up and down, a distinct *click* can be heard as the adjuster pin hits the tip of the valve stem.

VALVE TIMING

Punch marks are impressed adjacent to certain teeth on the crankshaft pinion, timing pinion, and camwheels to enable the owner to restore the valve timing correctly in the event of the camwheels being removed. Removal is, however, rarely necessary. Never attempt to alter the maker's valve timing. It is the best obtainable!

The correct valve timing for the various 1945–59 engines is shown in Figs. 54 and 55.

The Marking of the Timing Gears. The camwheels, intermediate gear, and the engine pinion, as previously mentioned, are all conveniently marked. Each camwheel has one *dot* mark. The engine pinion also has

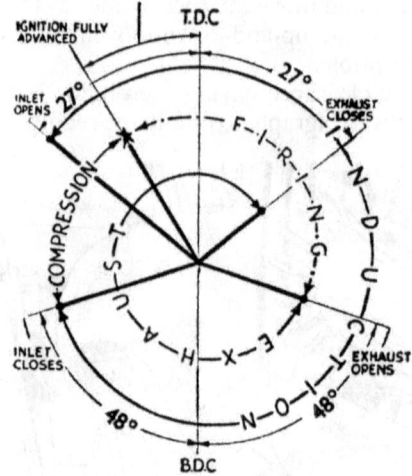

FIG. 54. VALVE TIMING DIAGRAM FOR 1945–59 MODELS
TR5, TR6 AND T110

When checking the valve timing the valve clearances
should be set to 0·020 in. (0·50 mm).

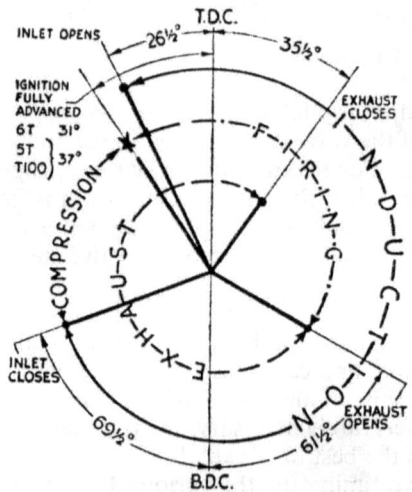

FIG. 55. VALVE TIMING DIAGRAM FOR 1945–59 MODELS
5T, 6T, T100, 3TA AND 5TA

This valve timing diagram also applies to the 1937–9 model 5T. On models
3TA and 5TA the ignition timing fully advanced is 35 degrees before T.D.C.
When checking the valve timing the valve clearances should be set to
0·020 in. (0·50 mm).

GENERAL MAINTENANCE: THE ENGINE

one dot mark. The intermediate gear, however, has two dot marks on adjacent teeth, a dot mark and a *dash* mark on two other adjacent teeth, and a single dot mark on a fifth tooth.

On Triumph models T110, T120, TR5 and TR6 the valve operation is correctly timed when the timing marks register as follows: the single dot mark on the engine pinion tooth comes between the adjacent dot marks on two intermediate gear teeth; the single dot mark between two teeth on the inlet camwheel registers with the single *dash* mark on an intermediate gear tooth; the single dot mark on the exhaust camwheel registers with the single dot mark on a tooth of the intermediate gear.

On Triumph models 5T, 6T, T100, 3TA and 5TA the valve operation is timed correctly when the above registering of the timing marks occurs, with the exception of the timing marks on the inlet camwheel and the intermediate gear. Here the single dot between two teeth on the inlet cam wheel registers with the single dot (not a dash mark) on a tooth of the intermediate gear.

As regards the direction of rotation of the timing gears, note that only the intermediate gear turns anti-clockwise when the engine pinion is moving in its normal direction of rotation.

IGNITION TIMING (MAGNETO)

Leave the magneto in position, but remove the timing cover and both sparking plugs; then proceed as follows—

Remove Magneto Gear. Unscrew the securing nut and screw into the gear centre with withdrawal tool DA50/1 supplied with the tool kit. With the tool in position, tighten the centre bolt and the gear will be withdrawn from the shaft. Set the contact-breaker points to 0·012 in. fully open.

Piston Positioning. Unscrew the rocker inspection caps; engage top gear and then rotate the rear wheel in the direction for forward travel, watching the valve operation in the left-hand (drive side) cylinder. When the inlet valve closes, gently rotate the rear wheel until the piston is at the top of the stroke (top dead centre or T.D.C.). The right piston position

1945–59 Magneto Ignition Timings

Model	TR5	TR6	T100	T110	T120
Maximum advance	$\frac{16}{18}$ in. (22 mm) before T.D.C.	$\frac{23}{64}$ in. (9·2 mm) before T.D.C.	$\frac{3}{8}$ in. (9·5 mm) before T.D.C.	$\frac{23}{64}$ in. (9·2 mm) before T.D.C.	$\frac{7}{16}$ in. (11 mm) before T.D.C.

can be felt with a timing stick when the rear wheel is rocked to and fro. On finding T.D.C. mark the lowest part of the timing stick which is visible at eye level and remove the stick, then make another mark (*see* "Ignition Timings Table") above the first mark. At this stage re-insert the timing stick into the cylinder and rotate the rear wheel backwards until the piston has fallen about 1 in.; then reverse the rotation and slowly bring the piston up to the desired mark on the timing stick. This eliminates any error due to backlash in the timing gears.

Positioning the Contact-Breaker. Take off the contact-breaker cover and advance the manual control lever on the handlebar (anti-clockwise)*:

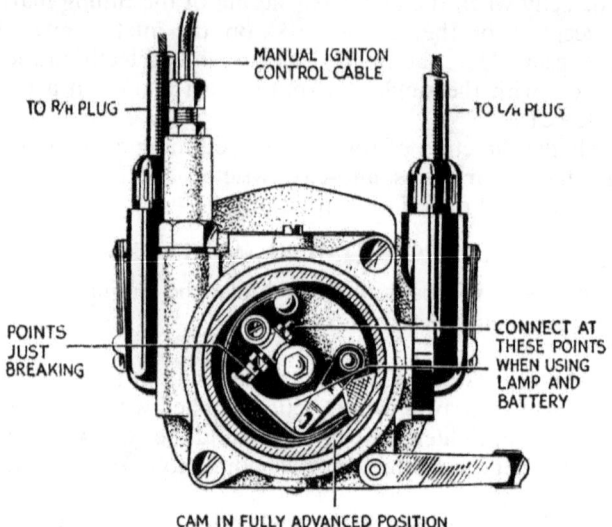

FIG. 56. LUCAS MAGNETO WITH CONTACT-BREAKER IN TIMING POSITION

Applies to 1945-9 models TR5, TR6, T100, T110, T120.

then rotate the contact-breaker until the points are in the upper position and just breaking (*see* Fig. 56). To tell the exact point of opening, slip a 0·0015 in. feeler gauge or a cellophane slip between the points and then rotate the contact-breaker when the gauge or cellophane will be released as soon as the points begin to open.

Replacing Magneto Gear. Keep the contact-breaker in the set position and fit the gear to the magneto shaft, seeing that both the shaft and the

* If an automatic timing device is fitted, wedge the unit lightly against the spring into the fully advanced position.

GENERAL MAINTENANCE: THE ENGINE 99

gear bore are free from oil; then tap the gear gently to engage the taper and fit and secure the washer and nut.

Finally check the timing again and, if correct, replace the timing cover, contact-breaker cover, sparking plugs, H.T. lead (*see* Fig. 56) and the four rocker inspection caps. If the timing is correct, join the plug leads, the one nearest the engine to the right-hand cylinder and the other lead to the left-hand cylinder.

IGNITION TIMING (COIL MODELS 5T AND 6T)

Replacing the Distributor, Adaptor and Coil. Assemble the distributor complete with the clamping lever to the adaptor and tighten the retaining bolt. Fit the adaptor to the crankcase with the clamping nut and bolt towards the crankcase and, with the slotted head pointing downwards, fit the lower retaining nut but do not tighten for the time being.

Clamp the coil on to the bracket and ensure that the two bolts are tight. Assemble the coil and bracket on to the upper two distributor adaptor studs and fit the remaining nuts. Tighten all three retaining nuts.

The distributor clamp nut and bolt should be sufficiently loose to allow the distributor to rotate for final positioning.

Replacing the Distributor Drive. The position of the distributor should be that which gives the easiest position for timing the ignition, and subsequent maintenance. Rotate the distributor body until the contact-breaker points are approximately at 11 o'clock when looking from the left hand of the machine; then tighten the lever clamping bolt in this position. To assist tightening, hold a long screwdriver against the slotted head of the clamping bolt from the under side of the engine. With the right-hand cylinder at T.D.C. on compression stroke, rotate the rotor arm clockwise until the contact-breaker points are just beginning to open, when the rotor arm is pointing to the rear of the machine. Hold the rotor arm in this position, slide the thrust washer, followed by the drive pinion, on to the distributor shaft so that the hole in the pinion boss lines up with the hole in the distributor shaft. Mesh the pinion into the nearest position on the mating pinion and slide the locking pin through the wheel and shaft, holding it in position by placing the circlip in the groove in the pinion boss. The distributor is then in the best position for final timing and adjustment of the contact-breaker points.

Setting Contact-breaker Points. To set the contact-breaker points, slacken the distributor clamp bolt and rotate the distributor slowly until the contact-breaker heel is on the peak of the cam lobe when the points should be separated. To adjust the points, slacken off the two screws securing the fixed contact plate and move the plate to give a 0·014 in.-0·016 in. gap between the contact points. Tighten up the screws and again check the gap adjustment.

100 THE BOOK OF THE TRIUMPH TWINS

Piston Positioning. Unscrew the rocker inspection caps, engage top gear and rotate the rear wheel in the direction of forward travel, watching the valve operation in the right-hand cylinder. When the inlet valve closes, continue to rotate the wheel slowly until the piston reaches the top of the stroke, that is, T.D.C. The correct piston position can be felt with the timing stick by rocking the rear wheel to and fro. When the true T.D.C. has been found, the 1954 model 6T should be timed with the piston

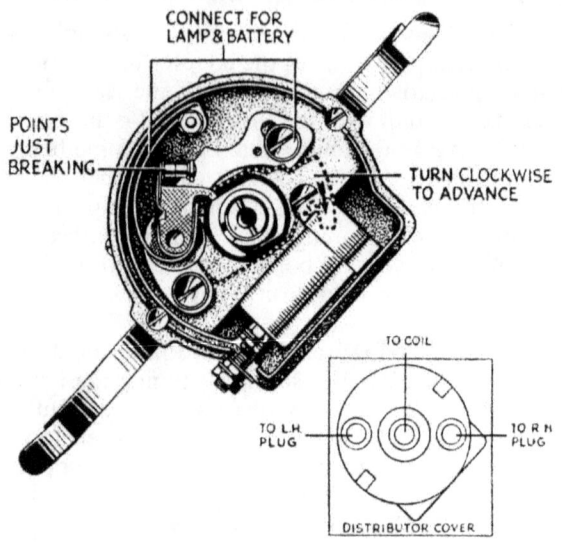

FIG. 57. LUCAS DISTRIBUTOR CONTACTS IN TIMING POSITION

in this position, but for the 1945–55 model 5T and the 1955 6T mark the lowest part of the timing stick which can be seen at eye level and remove the stick; then make another mark $\frac{1}{32}$ in. (0·80 mm) above the first mark. Now re-insert the timing stick and rotate the rear wheel backwards until the piston has fallen about $\frac{1}{4}$ in. (6 mm). Then reverse the rotation and bring the piston slowly up to the desired mark on the timing stick. This procedure eliminates any errors due to backlash in the timing gears.

Positioning of the Distributor. Standing on the right-hand side of the machine, place the left hand under the distributor, holding it in such a manner that it can be freely turned to the left or right. Then lean across the saddle or twinseat and rotate the distributor housing (contact-breaker points nearly vertical) until the points just open. Keeping the distributor in position, tighten up the clamp bolt and make another check.

To Check the Timing. Place a 0·0015-in. feeler gauge between the points. Turn the rotor arm against the springs on the *fully advanced* position when the feeler gauge should just be released. Then check that the lever clamp bolt is fully tightened. A long screwdriver should be held against the slotted head of the clamping bolt from the under side of the engine to prevent it rotating while the nut is being tightened.

When the timing has been carried out properly, join the plug leads, the lead nearest the engine to the left-hand cylinder and the opposite lead to the right-hand cylinder. Then fit the P.V.C. sheet over the distributor with the cut-away hole on the left-hand of the engine and fit the H.T. leads from the distributor cap into the cut-away.

IGNITION TIMING (COIL MODELS 3TA AND 5TA)

It is assumed that the distributor is in position ready for timing and that the gap between the contacts of the distributor (*see* Fig. 27) is correct. The makers recommend the following method of timing.

Timing Procedure. Fit, if available, a timing degree disc to the engine drive shaft and a rigid pointer to some part of the engine. Set to read 0 degrees with the right-hand piston exactly at T.D.C., with both the right tappets resting on the cams. Rotate the engine backwards about 10 degrees and then carefully move it forward so that the degree disc reading is 5 degrees before T.D.C.

Alternatively insert a suitable piece of thin rod on the piston through the sparking plug hole to locate T.D.C. Mark the rod to indicate T.D.C. and scratch another mark $\frac{1}{64}$ in. above the first mark and then turn the engine backwards so that the piston travels down about $\frac{1}{4}$ in.; then carefully turn the engine forwards until the piston is exactly $\frac{1}{64}$ in. (0·40 mm) before T.D.C. If the low tension supply is connected to the distributor, switch on the ignition, and observe the ammeter which will show a discharge of about 4 amps when the contact-breaker points are closed. Rotate the distributor body until the contacts just open, which will be shown by the ammeter reading falling to zero. Keep the distributor in this position and tighten the clamping bolt. If the low tension supply is not connected, use a 0·0015 in. (0·05 mm) feeler gauge or piece of tissue paper to determine when the contacts are just about to open. Fit the distributor cap; the front cable should be connected to the right-hand sparking plug and the rear cable to the left-hand plug.

DECARBONIZING AND GRINDING-IN VALVES

The removal of carbon deposits is necessary only when the engine shows definite signs of requiring decarbonizing. The necessity for decarbonizing is indicated by a gradual falling off in power (especially on hills), a tendency for "pinking" (injurious to the engine), some loss of compression, rather noisy running, a somewhat "woolly" exhaust, more difficult starting, and a tendency for the sparking plugs to become dirty quickly. Under normal running conditions the engine will probably run at least 10,000 miles between the decarbonizing periods. Valve grinding can conveniently be done when decarbonizing, and the valves and their seats should always be inspected.

Note that *it is entirely unnecessary to remove the cylinder block each time the engine is decarbonized.* The makers strongly advise that the cylinder block is not disturbed unless it is proposed to fit new piston rings or do some other work on the engine which requires that the cylinder block be removed. Unless the piston rings are in bad condition, and engine compression has much deteriorated, the renewal of the piston rings is quite unnecessary and the engine will run more smoothly and give better service if the rings are not touched.

Prior to stripping down the engine for a top overhaul, clean the parts about to be removed thoroughly, using paraffin or a proprietary degreasing agent. Also obtain two boxes, one for the cylinder head and associated parts, and the other for nuts, washers, etc. This will avoid waste of time searching for lost parts during the assembly of the engine. If care is taken, decarbonizing is a straightforward and fairly simple job. Gasket sets are available for all Triumph Twins, and before commencing decarbonizing get the correct set for your own particular model.

Removing Cylinder Head (1937–9 Twin-cylinder Engines). Dismantling procedure in the case of the 1937–9 "Speed Twin" and "Tiger 100" engines is very straightforward. Just underneath the petrol tank there is a joint in the oil pipe to the gauge which makes it unnecessary to lift the instrument panel. Eight bolts secure the cylinder head. Four of these also pass through the rocker boxes. Turn the petrol tank over sideways a little to facilitate removal of the cylinder head bolts. Lift off the cylinder head complete with the rocker boxes from the cylinder block. Be careful not to lose the copper washers when removing the oil return pipes which connect to the cylinder head and push-rod cover tubes. When reassembling the rocker boxes, fit new gaskets and see that the tappets and push-rods are correctly located when replacing the cylinder head. Tighten down the cylinder head evenly, working from the centre outwards. A copper plate is fitted between the cylinder block and head and this does not require renewing except after big mileages. However, it is beneficial to anneal the plate by heating over a gas ring. After reassembly is complete, adjust the valve clearances, warm up the engine, and again check the nuts and bolts for tightness.

Removing Cylinder Head (All 1945–59 Models Except 3TA, 5TA). *Saddle* (where fitted): remove the front bolt and tie back the saddle clear of the petrol tank.

Twinseat: this unit must be removed by slackening the two upper

GENERAL MAINTENANCE: THE ENGINE 103

suspension unit fixing bolts and removing the front bracket to frame bolt.

Petrol Tank: turn off the petrol tap or taps and disconnect the petrol pipes. Unscrew the four tank securing bolts when the tank can be removed. Take care not to lose the rubber tank-pads.

Exhaust System: slacken the exhaust-pipe finned clip bolts, remove the pipe to bracket bolts, the silencer steady to frame nut and the silencer hanger bolts. Remove each pipe and silencer as an assembly. (On models

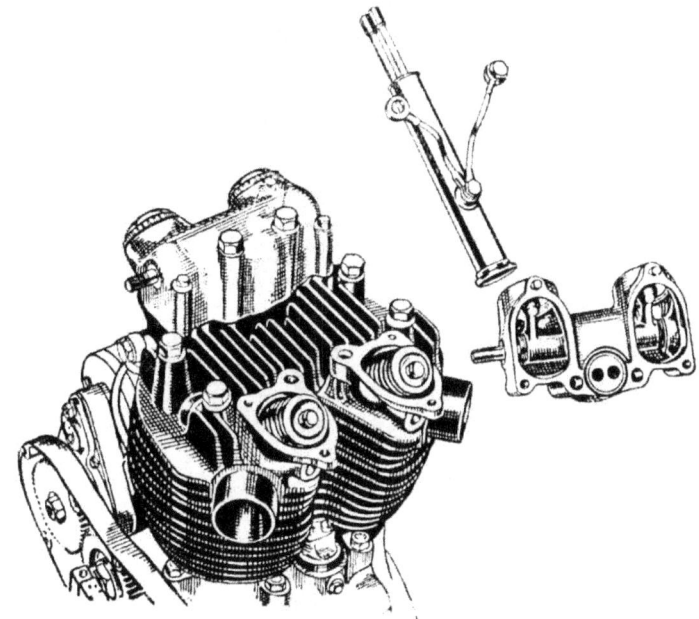

FIG. 58. 1937-9 ENGINE PARTLY STRIPPED SHOWING EXHAUST VALVE DETAILS

TR5 and TR6 the branch pipe clip bolt should also be slackened and the near-side pipe and silencer taken off first.)

Torque Stays: remove the nuts securing the stays to the cylinder head bolts and slacken off the stays to frame bolt when the stays can be disconnected.

Electrical Equipment: disconnect the H.T. leads and remove the sparking plugs.

Carburettor—Amal: remove the air cleaner connexion and remove the two flange nuts. Withdraw the carburettor from the fixing studs and tie it to the frame. If it is desired to clean the unit, unscrew the knurled ring securing the throttle and air slides and take away the mixing chamber assembly. Carefully tie the slide assembly to the frame, out of harm's way.

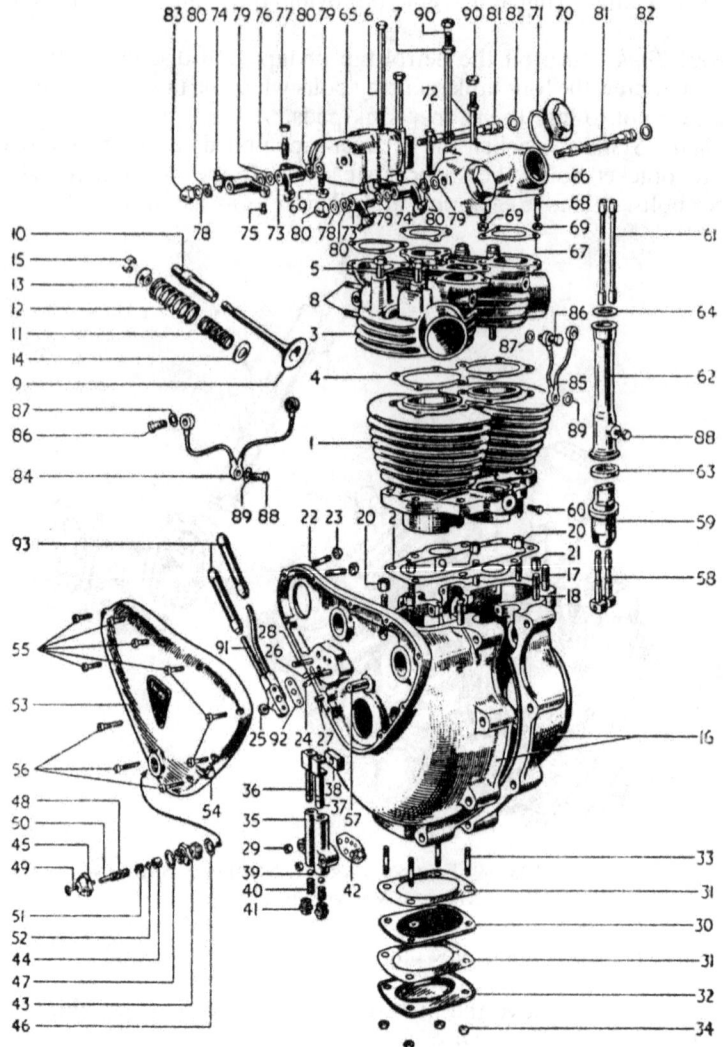

Fig. 59. Showing Details of the Engine on Model 6T

Except for slight differences the engine illustrated is the same on 1945-59 models 5T, T100, T110, T120, TR5 and TR6. A key to the numbered parts is on page 105.

(*By courtesy of the Triumph Engineering Co., Ltd.*)

GENERAL MAINTENANCE: THE ENGINE

Carburettor—S.U.: remove the air cleaner connexion and vent pipe from the carburettor. Unscrew the flange nuts and disconnect the throttle cable at the carburettor body when the carburettor can be removed.

Rocker Feed Pipe: unscrew the acorn nuts securing the rocker oil-feed pipe banjos to the rocker spindles and then ease the pipe off the spindles.

Rocker Drain Pipes: remove the adaptor bolts at the cylinder head only.

Rocker Boxes: first unscrew and remove the four centre bolts which secure the rocker boxes and cylinder head to the block. The next operation is to remove the *four nuts* (six nuts on models TR6, T110 and T120) holding the rocker boxes to cylinder head *before* removing the four small

---

KEY TO FIG. 59

1. Cylinder block
2. Cylinder base washer
3. Cylinder head
4. Cylinder head gasket
5. Short bolt
6. Medium bolt
7. Long bolt
8. Inlet manifold stud
9. Valve
10. Valve guide
11. Valve inner spring
12. Valve outer spring
13. Valve collar
14. Valve spring cup
15. Valve split cotter
16. Crankcase
17. Cylinder base stud
18. Cylinder base stud (dowel)
19. Nut for stud
20. Nut for stud
21. Cylinder base stud dowel
22. Magneto to crankcase stud
23. Nut for stud
24. Oil junction block stud
25. Nut for stud
26. Oil junction block dowel
27. Timing cover dowel
28. Oil pump stud
29. Nut for stud
30. Oil filter
31. Filter cover joint washer
32. Filter cover
33. Filter cover stud
34. Nut for stud
35. Oil pump body
36. Oil pump feed plunger
37. Oil pump scavenge plunger
38. Oil pump slider block
39. Oil pump ball valve
40. Oil pump valve spring
41. Oil pump plug
42. Oil pump washer
43. Oil release valve body
44. Release valve piston
45. Release valve cap
46. Body washer
47. Cap washer
48. Main spring
49. Indicator shaft
50. Rubber tube
51. Auxiliary spring
52. Shaft nut
53. Timing cover
54. Timing cover plug
55. Short screw
56. Long screw
57. Intermediate wheel spindle
58. Tappet
59. Guide block
60. Lock screw
61. Push-rod
62. Cover tube
63. Lower washer
64. Upper washer
65. Inlet rocker-box
66. Exhaust rocker-box
67. Rocker-box gasket
68. Rocker-box stud
69. Nut for stud
70. Inspection cap
71. Cap washer
72. Rocker-box bolt
73. R.H. valve rocker
74. L.H. valve rocker
75. Rocker ball pin
76. Adjusting pin
77. Lock-nut
78. Thrust washer
79. Thrust washer
80. Spring washer
81. Rocker spindle
82. Spindle seal
83. Dome nut
84. Oil drain pipe for inlet rockers
85. Oil drain pipe for exhaust rockers
86. Adaptor (head to pipe)
87. Washer
88. Adaptor (pipe to cover tube)
89. Washer
90. Torque stay nut
91. Pipes and block (oil tank to engine)
92. Oil pipe block washer
93. Oil pipe connexion (rubber)

rocker box bolts. *Failure to observe this warning may result in broken cylinder head lugs.* When all fixings have been unscrewed, remove the rocker boxes.

Cylinder Head: unscrew the remaining four holding-down bolts, when the head can be lifted off the block.

Push-rods and Covers: remove.

Replacing Cylinder Head (1945–55 Models 3T, 5T, T100, T110 and TR5).
Inlet Push-rods and Cover: first fit the lower rubber oil seals over both tappet blocks. Now assemble the inlet push-rods and cover to the tappets and block. Ensure that the drain pipes are fitted at this stage.

Cylinder Head: fit the copper gasket to the cylinder block and then fit the head complete with manifold. Enter and screw down the four short bolts, but do not fully tighten.

Inlet Rocker Box: grease the rocker box gaskets and upper push-rod cover washer and assemble to the rocker box. Turn the engine over until both inlet push-rods are nearly level and then assemble the rocker box to the cylinder head and push-rod cover. Check that the gaskets have not been misplaced and then enter the two short rocker box holding-down bolts and firmly screw down. Fit and tighten the two rocker box to cylinder head nuts. *The fitting of the bolts must precede the nuts.* If the valve seats have been re-cut and the valve faces re-ground, it is a good plan to slacken back the rocker adjuster before fitting the rocker box.

Exhaust Rocker Box: fit the push-rods and cover to the tappet and block (drain pipes fitted). Fit the exhaust rocker box in exactly the same manner as the inlet one.

Rocker Oil-drain Adaptors: ensure that the oil-drain adaptor bolts are clean and then fit a copper washer to each. Slide another copper washer between the oil-drain banjo, and insert the adaptor and tighten. Care should be exercised when tightening into an alloy head (TR5 and T100).

Cylinder Head Holding Bolts: position the remaining four bolts (the torque stay bolts to the rear) and screw down until a grip is felt. All eight bolts should now be evenly tightened but do not use excessive force on the spanner. The actual force required is 18 foot-pounds; if tightened beyond this figure distortion may take place.

Torque Stays: replace the stays to the engine bolts and securely tighten the nuts and clip bolts.

Rocker Oil-feed Pipe: place one copper washer on each rocker spindle; fit the oil pipe banjos over the spindles, followed by another copper washer and the two domed nuts. When tightening the nuts, steady the oil pipe at the spindles to prevent it turning, otherwise a broken joint may result.

Tappets: re-set the tappets and replace the rocker inspection caps complete with new washers, to the rocker box.

GENERAL MAINTENANCE: THE ENGINE

Carburettor—Amal: if the carburettor slides have been removed, replace them at this stage and after screwing down the knurled fixing ring, test the slide operation by working the controls. Position the flange washer to the manifold (TR5 and T100 flange washer, Tufnol block and flange washer). Also fit a new "O" ring seal in the groove in the carburettor body. Then fit the carburettor to the studs. Connect up the filter connexion; fit the flange nuts and washers; tighten nuts.

Carburettor—S.U.: fit the flange washer and assemble the carburettor to the manifold, connect the air filter connexion and vent pipe. Fit and tighten the two flange nuts. Assemble the throttle cable to the carburettor body and test operation.

Exhaust System: replace the exhaust pipes and silencers as an assembly and ensure that all securing bolts are well tightened.

Petrol Tank: replace the tank to the frame and ensure that a rubber pad is fitted at each side of the connexion. Connect up the petrol pipes.

Saddle or Twinseat: position to frame and tighten the fixing bolts.

Testing: check the petrol tank for fuel content, turn on the petrol tap, set the controls and start the engine. Run for a limited time until the engine is warm and then set the slow running on the carburettor (*see* page 16). Finally check over all engine nuts and bolts.

Replacing Cylinder Head (1956–9 Models T110, T120 and TR6). *Pushrod Cover Tubes:* fit new rubber washers to the tappet blocks and new silicone rubber washers to the top flange of the push-rod cover tubes. Position the tubes, with the notch on the bottom flange of each tube facing *away* from the crankshaft.

Cylinder Head: anneal the cylinder head gasket by heating cherry red and plunging into cold water. Place the gasket in position, followed by the cylinder head. Now insert the four short head-to-barrel bolts. See that the push-rod cover tubes are in their correct positions and screw down the bolts. At this stage do not tighten them.

Inlet Rocker Box: place the push-rods in position and make sure that their lower ends seat on the tappets. Grease the paper joint washer and place it over the rocker box studs. Place the rocker box in position and see that the rocker ends engage with the push-rods. Insert the two rocker box-to-cylinder head bolts and tighten them down. Then secure the rocker box with the three nuts and washers.

Exhaust Rocker Box: use the same assembly procedure as for the inlet rocker box. Finally insert the four long cylinder head bolts (torque stay bolts at the rear) and tighten down the cylinder head. Tighten each bolt a few turns at a time, commencing from the centre bolts and moving diagonally across the cylinder head.

The remainder of the assembly work should be done exactly as described on page 106 from the paragraph "Torque Stays" to "Testing."

Removing Cylinder Head (Models 3TA and 5TA). *Petrol Tank:* turn off the petrol tap and disconnect the pipe at the union below the tap. Raise the twinseat (*see* Fig. 60) to obtain access to the rear bolt, and remove the two bolts and nuts which secure the petrol tank to the frame. Now remove the petrol tank.

Exhaust System: slacken the finned clips. Also remove the small bolts

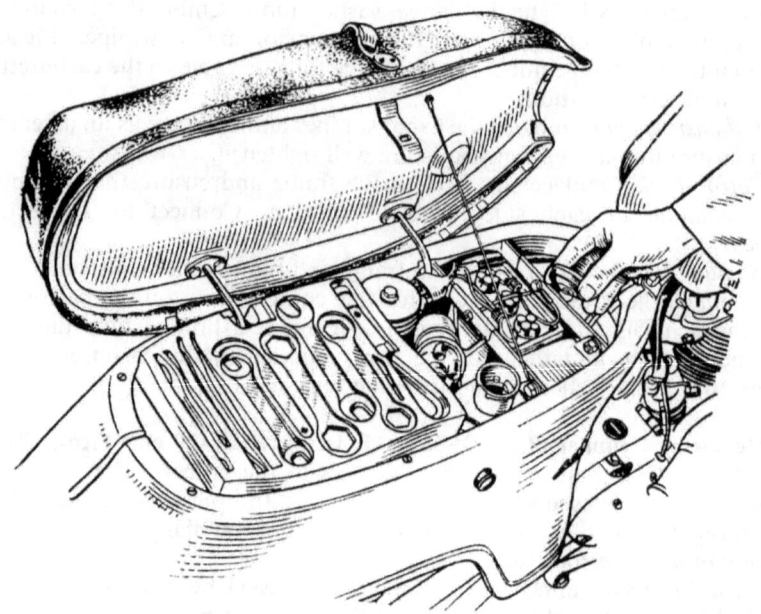

FIG. 60. THE TWINSEAT RAISED ON MODEL 3TA OR 5TA

On models 3TA and 5TA the oil tank and tool kit are both beneath the twinseat.

from the supporting stays and silencer hanger bolts. Remove each pipe and silencer as an assembly.

Amal Carburettor: remove the air cleaner connexion and unscrew the two flange nuts. Withdraw the carburettor from the fixing studs and tie it to the frame. Should you desire to clean the instrument (*see* page 20), unscrew the knurled ring securing the throttle and air slides and take away the mixing chamber assembly. Carefully tie the slide assembly to the frame so that it is out of the way.

Torque Stays: remove the engine torque stays.

Rocker Oil Feed Pipes: remove the acorn nuts and long bolts which secure the oil feed pipes to the rocker box.

GENERAL MAINTENANCE: THE ENGINE

Rocker Boxes: unscrew the four nuts which secure the rocker boxes to the cylinder head *before* removing the *four* Philip screws and the four long bolts which also secure the cylinder head to the cylinder block. Lift out the push-rods.

The Cylinder Head: unscrew the four short cylinder head-to-block bolts, lift the cylinder head a little way, and then lift the push-rod cover tubes and swing their upper ends outwards in order to lift off the cylinder head.

Replacing Cylinder Head (Models 3TA and 5TA).
Cylinder Head: fit new rubber washers inside the bottom of the push-rod cover tubes and place them over the tappet blocks but not fully home. Anneal the cylinder head gasket by heating to cherry red and plunging it into cold water. Fit new silicone rubber washers in the groove in the cylinder head and place the head in position, swinging the tops of the push-rod cover tubes outwards to place the head in position. Make sure that the push-rod cover tubes are pressed well down and that their upper ends are seating properly in the grooves in the cylinder head. Fit the four short outer cylinder-head bolts and washers and screw them down finger-tight.

Inlet Rocker Box: place the push-rods in position with the cupped ends uppermost and make sure that they are located in the tappets. Grease the joint washer and place it on the rocker box, over the studs. Place the rocker box in position and make sure that the rockers engage with the push-rods. Secure the rocker box with the Philip screws and two nuts.

Exhaust Rocker Box: use a similar assembly procedure as for the inlet rocker box. Now insert the four long cylinder-head bolts and washers (torque stay bolts in the front) and tighten down the eight cylinder-head bolts, starting from the inner bolts and working diagonally across the cylinder head.

Rocker Oil Feed Pipes: fit the long bolts and acorn nuts, complete with annealed copper washers at the bolt heads, under the banjo union and under the nut.

Torque Stays: replace and secure the torque stays.

Amal Carburettor: check that the throttle slide works freely in the carburettor. Fit a new "O" ring to the carburettor, and a paper washer and the insulating block to the manifold. Tighten the nuts evenly.

Valve Clearances: adjust the valve clearances as described on page 93, and replace the inspection caps with new joint washers.

Plug Leads: replace the sparking plug leads. The lead from the front of the distributor connects to the right sparking plug, and the lead from the rear of the distributor to the left sparking plug.

Exhaust System: replace the exhaust pipes and silencers.

Petrol Tank: replace the petrol tank and re-connect the petrol pipe to the cap.

Testing: start up the engine, remove the oil tank filler cap (*see* Fig. 60)

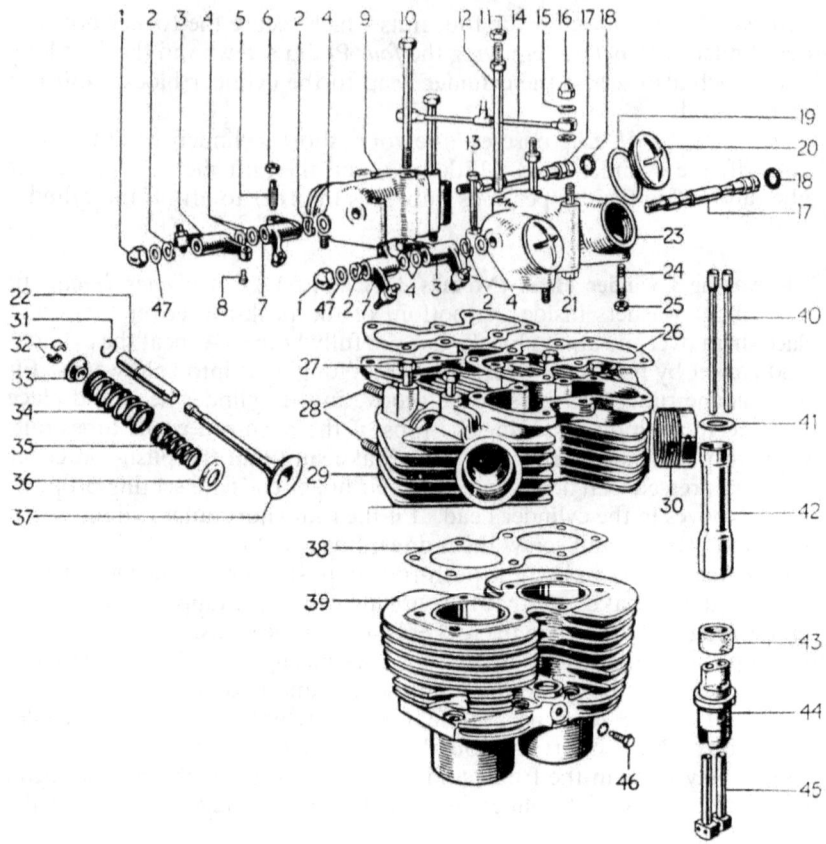

FIG. 61. SHOWING DETAILS OF THE UPPER PART OF THE ENGINE FITTED TO MODELS 3TA AND 5TA

(By courtesy of the Triumph Engineering Co., Ltd.)

1. Rocker spindle nut
2. Thackeray washer
3. L.H. valve rocker
4. Thrust washer
5. Rocker adjuster
6. Locking nut
7. R.H. valve rocker
8. Rocker ball pin
9. Inlet rocker-box
10. Bolt to cylinder block
11. Torque stay nut
12. Bolt for torque stay
13. Phillips head screw
14. Oil feed pipe
15. Fibre washer
16. Domed nut
17. Rocker spindle
18. Spindle seal
19. Fibre washer
20. Inspection cap
21. Hollow bolt
22. Valve guide
23. Exhaust rocker-box
24. Stud
25. Nut
26. Rocker-box gasket
27. Bolt to cylinder block
28. Manifold stud
29. Cylinder head
30. Exhaust adaptor
31. Circlip
32. Split collet
33. Top collar
34. Valve outer spring
35. Valve inner spring
36. Bottom collar
37. Inlet valve
38. Cylinder head gasket
39. Cylinder block
40. Push-rod
41. Silicone rubber washer
42. Cover tube
43. Rubber washer
44. Tappet block
45. Tappet
46. Locking bolt
47. Thrust washer

GENERAL MAINTENANCE: THE ENGINE

and place a finger over the hole in the return pipe for a few seconds to divert extra oil to the rocker gear. Run the engine for 5-10 minutes, allow it to cool, and check the nuts and bolts for tightness. Do not overtighten by using extra-long spanners. The leverage afforded by the spanners provided in the tool-kit is quite sufficient.

Removing the Carbon. Care and thoroughness in decarbonizing well repays the labour expended and, after all, you are preparing the engine for about another 10,000 miles, running without complaining!

To remove carbon deposits from the cylinder head use a proprietary scraper or a screwdriver. The scraper is preferably a flat round-headed type. The author finds that quite a useful tool for helping to scrape off the carbon from the curved walls of the combustion chambers is a small electrical screwdriver. Great care must always be taken not to damage the valve seatings when chipping off carbon in the immediate vicinity of the seats. It is safest to keep the valves temporarily in position prior to inspecting the seats and valve faces and grinding-in the valves if necessary. Remove all traces of carbon from the interior surfaces and do not forget the ports (especially the exhaust ports) and the sparking plug holes. Carbon forms less easily on a polished surface and it is a good plan to polish the combustion chamber surfaces of a cast-iron head with some fine emery cloth, but this should be done *before* the valves are removed, and afterwards all traces of abrasive must be cleaned away with a rag and paraffin. *On no account use emery cloth where an aluminium-alloy head is used.* Also take special care not to use excessive pressure with the scraper and thereby deeply scratch the combustion chamber walls.

The pistons are both made of a light-alloy and are therefore vulnerable to careless decarbonizing. Carefully clean away the carbon deposits from the piston crowns. When removing the carbon each piston should, of course, be placed at T.D.C. The carbon can be removed with a proprietary scraper, a screwdriver, or a blunt knife. Never use emery cloth or any abrasive to polish the piston crowns. If abrasive particles get past the top piston rings no end of damage may be caused to the cylinder bores. Some novices are apt to overlook this vital point. If the pistons are not removed (rarely necessary) and the cylinder block is left undisturbed (normally recommended), do not remove the slight carbon ring deposits on the piston crown circumferences. They form an excellent oil seal and can cause no harm, provided the deposits are not thick. As is the case with a light-alloy cylinder head, be particularly careful not to scratch the piston crowns deeply when chipping off the carbon. By holding the scraper at a suitable angle, using the right type of scraper, and not using excessive force, this can be avoided. After removing all traces of carbon, clean both piston crowns with a clean rag damped in paraffin, and cover up the mouths of the cylinder bores.

To Remove the Valves. As has already been mentioned on page 102, the valves should all be removed and inspected when decarbonizing. A close examination of the valve seats should also be made. To remove the valves it is desirable to use a good valve spring compressor such as the tool shown in Fig. 62. It can be obtained from a Triumph dealer or an

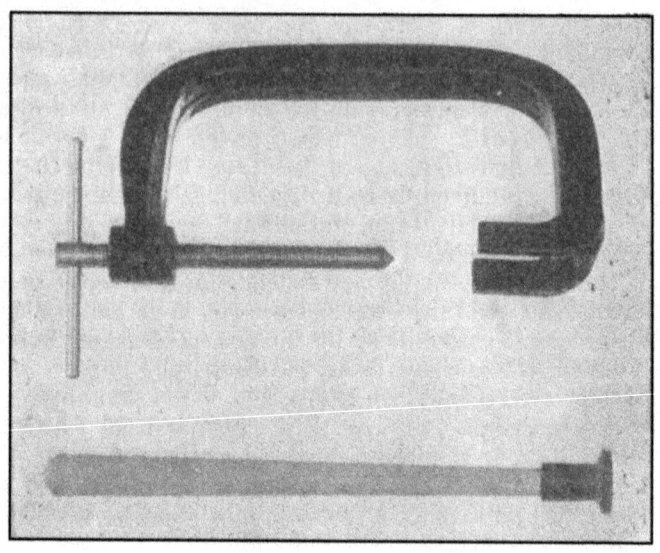

FIG. 62. TWO USEFUL PROPRIETARY TOOLS FOR THE VALVES

Above is shown a sturdy valve spring compressor, and below a suction type valve grinding tool

accessory firm. Compress valve spring with the valve spring compressor, with the forked end of the tool contacting the valve spring top collar. After turning the tommy bar or wing nut of the compressor several turns, loosen the split collet by delivering a sharp tap with a hammer on the forked end of the tool. The split collet halves can then be eased away with a narrow screwdriver or similar tool. Release the valve spring compressor and withdraw the top collar, the inner and outer valve springs, and the valve itself. Deal with each of the four valves similarly, and be careful not to mix up the valves. They must be replaced exactly as removed. The inlet and exhaust valves are marked "IN" and "EX" to assist correct replacement.

Examining Valve Springs. After a considerable mileage the valve springs lose their tension, and their length decreases. If a new duplex spring is available, check the free length of each inner and outer spring with the corresponding springs of the new duplex valve spring. If a new

GENERAL MAINTENANCE: THE ENGINE   113

duplex spring is not available, check the free length of the inner and outer springs. The probability is that if one valve spring has deteriorated, the others have also and where a valve spring is found unsatisfactory it is the best policy to replace all four duplex springs with a new set. They are not expensive, but are most important.

On all 1945–59 engines except models 3TA and 5TA the correct free length of the outer valve spring is 2·031 in. The free length of the inner valve spring is 1·625 in. On a model 3TA or 5TA the respective free lengths are $1\frac{5}{8}$ in. and $1\frac{9}{16}$ in. or $1\frac{1}{2}$ in. and $1\frac{21}{32}$ in. respectively.

Insert each valve stem in its guide and check for play by attempting to move the valve sideways. If there is much wear and scuffing, replace the valve. A new valve will, of course, require to be ground-in. A valve stem often wears more than its guide, and a distinct shoulder may be felt near the neck of the valve. In this case fitting a new valve will probably remedy slackness without fitting a new valve guide.

Replacing Valve Guides. To remove an old guide place a shoulder drift into the valve guide from the inside of the combustion chamber and drive out. When fitting the new guide, grease the outer diameter and drive into the cylinder head from the top. Always use a shoulder drift when doing this operation, and drive in the guide very carefully to prevent any damage being done.

Grinding-in the Valves. Use the suction tool shown in Fig. 62 or alternatively a metal grinding-in tool which can be secured to the tip of the valve stems. To grind-in a valve (see that it is the correct one), holding the cylinder head firmly on a bench or table, clean both the valve seat and the valve face. Smear with a piece of rag or the finger tip a thin film of fine carborundum grinding paste (coarse at first if handling a valve seat and valve face which are badly pitted) on the bevelled valve face. Replace the valve in its guide minus the valve spring. Be careful not to interchange the inlet and exhaust valves which are marked as previously mentioned.

When grinding-in a valve, a light pressure on the grinding tool is required and care must be taken not to rock the valve, particularly if the valve guide is slightly worn. Rotate the valve about a *third of a turn* in one direction and then an equal amount in the opposite direction, pausing every few oscillations to raise the valve from its seat and turn about 180 degrees. Cease grinding-in when no "cut" can be felt (and the valve begins to "sing") and put some more grinding paste on the bevelled edge of the valve face if, after cleaning the valve in paraffin, some pitting is still visible.

Proceed with grinding-in until both the valve bevelled face and seat have a matt metallic surface uniformly over an appreciable width (line contact is not sufficient) and there are no pitting marks left on the valve or its seating after wiping the paste off. Note that excessive grinding-in after a good seating has been effected, or in any circumstances, can lead to the valve becoming "pocketed" which causes an appreciable decline in the power output of the engine. Always take a cylinder block with very badly pitted valve seats to a Triumph dealer for valve seat refacing. Before making a final examination of the valve and its seating, thoroughly clean them both with a paraffin- or petrol-soaked rag to ensure that there is no trace of abrasive left. Afterwards put the rag in the dustbin.

Refitting the Valves. After grinding-in the valves, assemble them in their correct positions in the cylinder head. Valve stem end-caps are not provided. See that all parts are quite clean, and fit each valve in the following manner. Smear the valve stem with some engine oil and insert the valve stem in its guide and, holding the valve head against its seat, turn the cylinder head on its side, replace the lower spring cup over the valve guide, next the duplex valve spring, and finally the outer collar. Now, with the valve spring compressor, compress the valve spring until the split collet can be fitted into the outer collar and around the valve stem cut-away. Make sure that the collet beds down properly. The application of a little grease to the inside of a split collet helps it to stick on the valve stem until the duplex spring is released by removing the pressure exerted by the valve spring compressor tool. After releasing the tool, tap the stem head of the valve smartly to ensure correct bedding down of the split collet.

Removing the Cylinder Block (All Engines). Where cylinder block removal is necessary (not often advised), unscrew the eight nuts which hold it to the crankcase studs. Also secure the tappets in the cylinder block by pressing a rubber wedge between the tappets (*see* Fig. 66). Avoid using excessive force when doing this. Now gently lift the cylinder block off the two pistons. Before removing the block completely it is a good plan to raise the block some distance and then place a clean cloth over the mouth of the crankcase. This will prevent any dirt or piece of broken piston ring (in the event of one being damaged) entering the crankcase. It is extremely difficult to extract dirt or pieces of metal from the crankcase. When the cylinder block is removed test the connecting-rods for vertical play at B.D.C.

Examining and Removing the Piston Rings. The piston rings are responsible for maintaining good compression. They must therefore be full of spring, free in their grooves, and set with their slots opposite to each other (i.e., at 120 degrees in the case of the three-ring pistons provided on all twin-cylinder engines). If all three rings are bright all the way round, they are obviously being nicely polished and satisfactorily contact the cylinder bores, and should be left alone. If the rings are discoloured at some points they are not making good contact with the bores, thereby causing gas to blow past them. Possibly some rings are stuck in their grooves with burnt oil and will function correctly if the piston ring grooves are cleaned. Should the rings be scored, are vertically loose in their grooves, or have lost their proper tension, renewal of the rings concerned should be effected.

Piston rings are made of cast-iron and are small in section. They must therefore always be handled with extreme care. The bottom ring on each piston is a scraper ring and this is particularly vulnerable to damage. Piston rings cannot safely be opened out wider than will enable them to

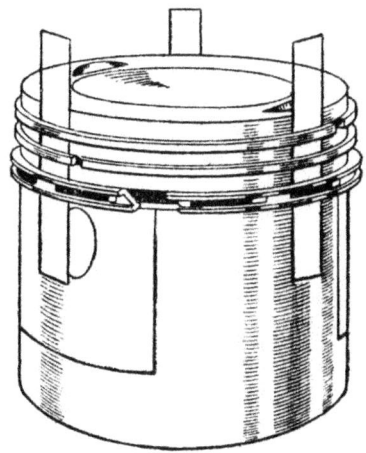

FIG. 63. A SAFE METHOD OF REMOVING
AND FITTING PISTON RINGS

Note the slotted scraper ring below the two compression rings. This ring is very fragile. Some rings are marked on one face "TOP" (see text).

slip over the crowns of the pistons. Excessively wide opening out of any piston ring will cause it to snap immediately. To remove or replace used rings, or fit new piston rings, it is best to insert small strips of sheet-metal (about $\frac{3}{8}$ in. wide and 2 in. long) in the manner shown in Fig. 63. Be careful to note the order in which piston rings are removed so as to ensure their being correctly replaced. When fitting piston rings, thoroughly clean the grooves into which they fit, as any deposit left at the back of new rings forces them out and makes them too tight a fit. Paraffin will usually loosen stuck rings.

When renewing the piston rings, always fit rings supplied by a Triumph dealer or a firm handling Triumph spares. Piston rings are made to extremely fine limits. It is particularly important to note that on all engines the second compression ring (i.e. the centre ring) has the word "TOP" etched on one face as shown in Fig. 64. This ring face must always face *towards the piston crown*. The face is tapered, hence the importance of the ring being correctly fitted on all 1945–59 engines. On 1945–55 T100, T110 and TR5 engines a *chrome* taper-faced top compression ring is also fitted and the taper face is marked "TOP." This taper face must also face towards the crown of the piston. The ring can be easily identified by its bright chrome appearance. On later 1956–9 engines (except on models 3TA and 5TA) two taper-faced compression rings (neither with a chrome

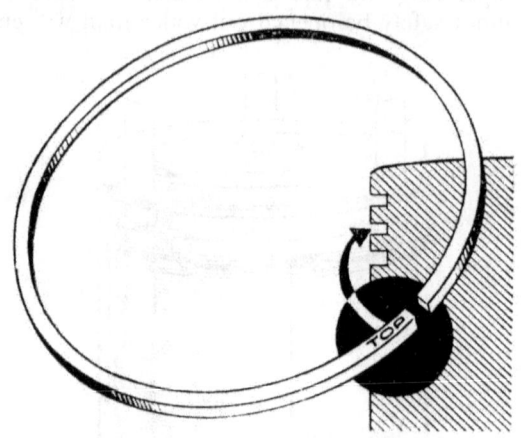

Fig. 64. Where Only One Taper-faced Piston Ring is Provided, It Must Always be Fitted Like This

finish) are provided and both must be fitted with the marking "TOP" uppermost.

Before fitting used piston rings do not forget to scrape off all carbon from the backs of the rings and from the ends of the rings. Also clean out the oil drain holes in the scraper-ring grooves. To clean the piston ring grooves it is a good plan to use an old broken ring and insert the broken end into the groove and work it round the circumference.

Checking the Gap of New Piston Rings. Before fitting a new piston ring, check its gap in the lowest part of the cylinder block bore. For checking purposes the piston ring should lie square to the bore. To ensure this, place the bottom of the piston skirt on to the ring and ease it about $\frac{1}{2}$ in. down the bore. With a feeler gauge check the gap.

On all engines except those of models 3TA and 5TA the correct compression ring gap (new) is 0·010 in. (minimum) and 0·014 in. (maximum). On model 3TA (350 c.c.) the correct compression ring gap is 0·008 in. and 0·010 in. (minimum and maximum respectively). On model 5TA (500 c.c.) the correct minimum and maximum compression ring gaps are 0·010 in. and 0·014 in. respectively. The correct scraper ring gap (new) on all engines except those of models 3TA and 5TA is: minimum (500 c.c.) 0·007 in.; maximum (500 c.c.) 0·011 in. On 650 c.c. engines the minimum and maximum scraper ring gaps are 0·010 in. and 0·014 in. respectively. The scraper ring gaps (new) on models 3TA and 5TA are identical to the

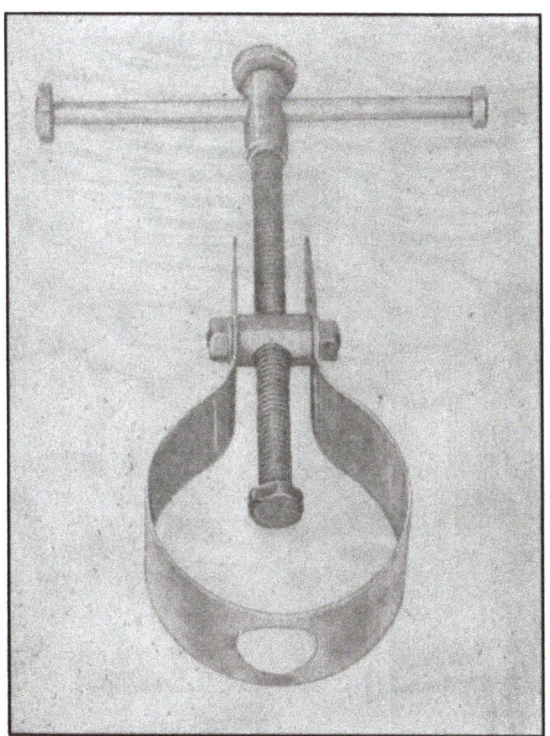

FIG. 65. PROPRIETARY TOOL FOR PRESSING GUDGEON-PIN IN OR OUT

Note the three different size pressure-pads on the ends of the tommy-bar and the pressure screw. They, of course, fit different size gudgeon-pins.

compression ring gaps on models 3TA and 5TA. If the gap of a new ring is less than the minimum specified figure, clamp the ring between two wooden blocks in a vice and *very* carefully file one of the diagonal ends slightly. If a new ring is a tight fit in the ring groove, rub down one side of the ring (not a face marked "TOP") on a sheet of fine carborundum paper laid on a sheet of plate glass.

Removing the Pistons (All Engines). Piston removal is seldom necessary or advisable. The following is the procedure to use for removing each piston. Remove both circlips from the piston bosses after first checking that the mouth of the crankcase is completely covered with a cloth. Each circlip must be renewed after removal. This is important. To remove each

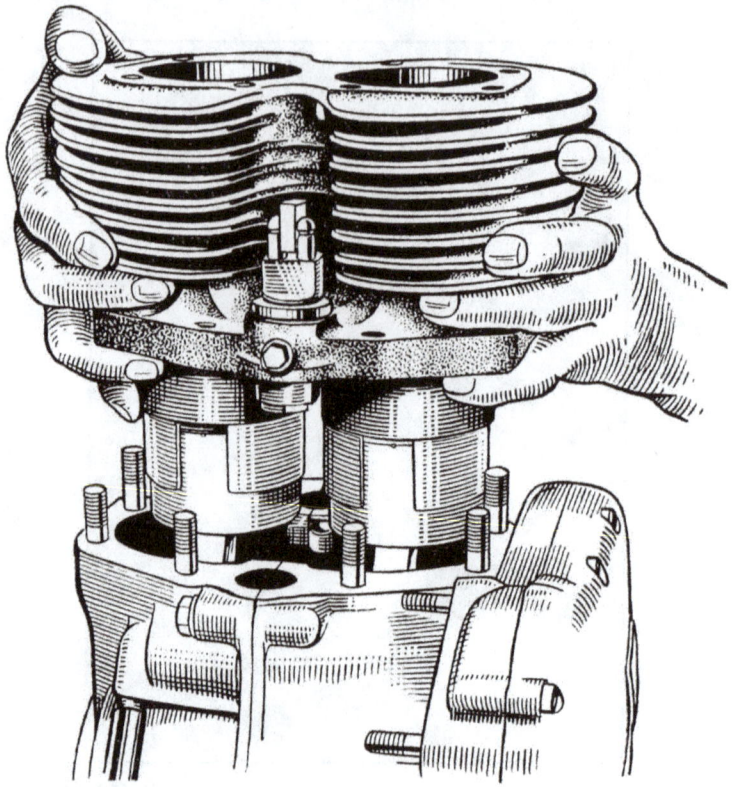

FIG. 66. LOWERING THE CYLINDER BLOCK OVER THE TWO PISTONS

Note the rubber wedge inserted between the tappets to prevent the tappets falling into the crankcase. Also note the two clips fitted around the piston rings.

circlip, use a small screwdriver or a pointed instrument such as the tang end of a file.

The gudgeon-pin is a fairly tight fit in the piston bosses (especially on a new engine). After removing both circlips use a proprietary tool such as that shown in Fig. 65 for pressing out the gudgeon-pin. Alternatively use a suitable diameter punch and light hammer to knock out the pin. If this method is used it is essential to support the piston firmly on the side opposite that where the hammer is applied. Failure to provide good support can cause an excessive side-stress to be imposed on the

GENERAL MAINTENANCE: THE ENGINE

connecting-rod. Should any difficulty be experienced in removing a gudgeon-pin, warm the piston by wrapping a cloth round the piston after immersing the cloth in hot water and wringing it out.

Replacing the Pistons. When replacing a piston see that you fit it to the correct connecting-rod the right way round. Oil the small-end bush of the connecting-rod and position the piston with one *new* circlip fitted. From the opposite side press or tap the gudgeon-pin (which should also be oiled) home until its end abuts the circlip already fitted. Then fit the remaining *new* circlip. Make sure that both circlips are fully bedded down in the piston grooves. Lubricate the piston rings and position the rings so that their gaps are correctly positioned (*see* page 116).

Re-fitting the Cylinder Block. Grease the washer for the cylinder block base. If not perfect, fit a new washer. It is assumed that both pistons are near B.D.C. and that the inlet and exhaust tappets are in position in the tappet blocks. Place a rubber wedge (*see* Fig. 66) between each pair of tappet stems to prevent the tappets falling into the crankcase when fitting the cylinder block. Oil both cylinder block bores thoroughly, especially at their upper ends and then carefully lower the cylinder block over the pistons, which should have piston ring clips fitted as shown in Fig. 66, until the piston rings slide up into the two cylinder block bores.

While holding the cylinder block squarely, get an assistant to turn the engine over slowly so as to slide the two pistons up into the cylinder block bores. As the pistons enter the bores, the piston ring clips will fall clear and can be withdrawn over the connecting-rods. Guide the cylinder block over the crankcase studs and then remove the rubber wedges from the two pairs of tappets. Replace the eight spring washers and nuts securing the cylinder block to the crankcase studs, and tighten the nuts firmly and in a diagonal order. Tighten them all finger-tight first.

THE CONNECTING-ROD AND CRANKSHAFT ASSEMBLY

Internal details of the engines fitted to models 5T, 6T, T100, T110, T120, TR5, TR6 are shown in Fig. 67. The arrangement is considerably different on models 3TA and 5TA. Where a major overhaul involving the crankshaft and/or connecting-rod assembly is concerned, it is always best to have the work done by a competent mechanic at a Triumph repair workshop. Special tools and much skill are required. It is beyond the scope of this handbook to enter into the subject. If you have the tools and skill to tackle the work on a bench, you will find useful instructions included in the Triumph Official Instruction Manual. Trouble with the connecting-rod and crankshaft assembly is very unlikely to occur until a huge mileage has been completed, i.e. assuming that you handle your Triumph with reasonable care. The author hopes that you experience no serious trouble anywhere on your machine.

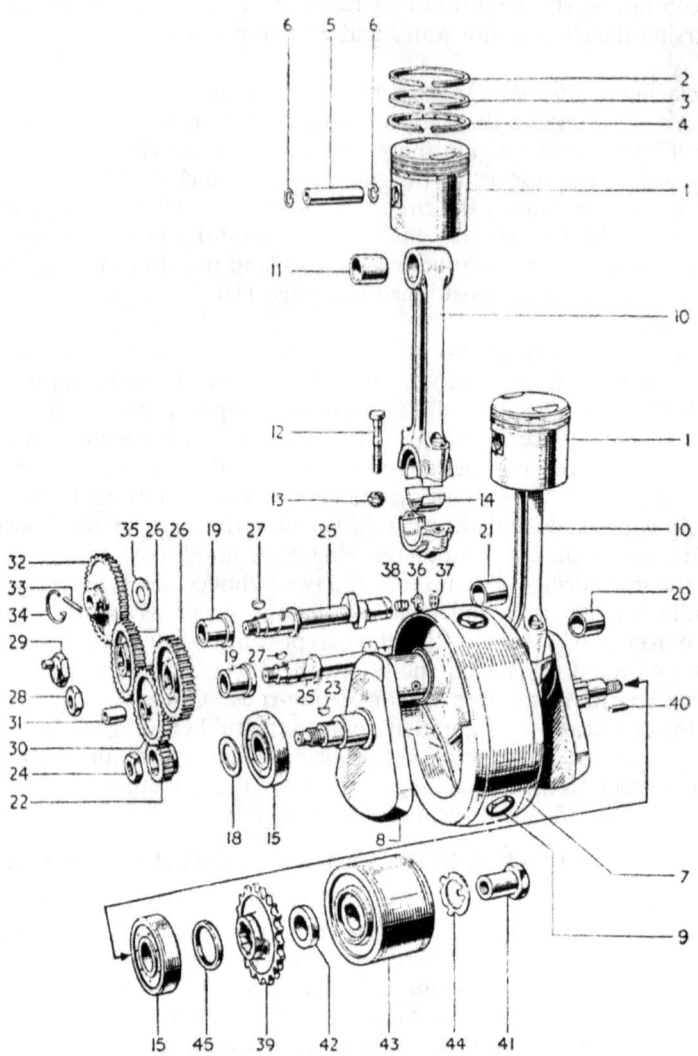

FIG. 67. SHOWING INTERNAL DETAILS OF THE ENGINE FITTED TO MODEL 6T

The general arrangement is similar on all the other engines, except on models 3TA and 5TA.

THE TWIST-GRIP

To Dismantle 1938–9 Twist-grip. To dismantle the twist-grip throttle control, peel back the rubber grip and withdraw the spring ring and washer. Then unscrew the cable stop and draw out the cable. Now draw off the grip. When doing this, be careful not to lose the small plunger and spring which provided the excellent click action.

When reassembling, the order is reversed, but it is necessary to revolve the grip when re-inserting the cable, so that the grip picks up the cable nipple and draws it into place.

Dismantling (All 1945–59 Models Except 1945–55 TR5). The damping of the rotor is controlled by a knurled adjuster nut fitted in the twist-grip. Damping can be increased by screwing in the adjuster until the friction is sufficient to hold the rotor sleeve in any position. If the damper is not sufficiently adjusted, the twist-grip will close immediately the hand is taken off, say, to give a road signal. Maintenance requires only light grease lubrication when assembled.

Cable Thimble. Unscrew the cable thimble from the twist-grip head; this is sometimes made easier by pulling on the cable close to the twist-grip. When unscrewed, the cable can be pulled out.

Rotor Sleeve. Pull back the twist-grip rubber and insert a thin blade behind retaining plate (2 Fig. 68); remove the circlip (3, Fig. 68) from the head and then withdraw the rotor sleeve assembly.

Head. Loosen the grub screw which holds the head to the handlebar and withdraw the head.

Assembly (All 1945–59 Models Except 1945–55 TR5). *Rotor Sleeve to Head.* Replace before assembling to the handlebar. Grease the rotor end

---

KEY TO FIG. 67

1. Piston
2. Top compression ring
3. Centre compression ring
4. Scraper ring
5. Gudgeon-pin
6. Circlip
7. Flywheel
8. Timing side crankshaft
9. Driving side crankshaft
10. Connecting-rod
11. Small-end bush
12. Big-end bolt
13. Nut for big-end bolt
14. Timing side bearing
15. Driving side bearing
18. Clamping washer
19. Camshaft timing side bush
20. Camshaft driving side bush
21. Bush for camshaft driving side (breather)
22. Timing pinion
23. Timing pinion key
24. Timing pinion nut
25. Camshaft
26. Camshaft wheel
27. Key for camshaft wheel
28. Exhaust camshaft nut
29. Inlet camshaft nut
30. Intermediate gearwheel
31. Bush for intermediate gearwheel
32. Distributor pinion
33. Pin for distributor pinion
34. Circlip for distributor pinion
35. Brass washer
36. Crankcase rotary valve
37. Rotary valve disc
38. Rotary valve spring
39. Engine sprocket
40. Rotor key
41. Sprocket and rotor nut
42. Clamping washer
43. Rotor
44. Locking washer

ring and fit the rotor sleeve into the head with the nipple housing close to the cable hole.

Slide the retaining plate into position and assemble the circlip to the head; then roll back the rubber grip. If fitting a new rubber, first wet the inside with petrol and then push it over the sleeve. This is, however, better done after the twist-grip has been fitted to the handlebar.

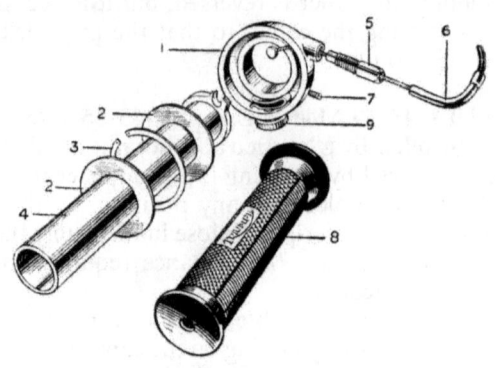

FIG. 68. TWIST-GRIP (ALL 1945–59 MODELS EXCEPT 1945–55 MODEL TR5)

1. Head assembly
2. Retaining plate
3. Circlip
4. Sleeve assembly
5. Cable thimble
6. Guide tube
7. Grub screw
8. Rubber grip
9. Friction adjuster screw

Twist-grip to Handlebar. Grease the swaged portion of the handlebar and slide on the twist-grip; lock in the desired position with the grub screw.

Throttle Cable. Hold the outer casing, pull the inner wire, gripping it close to the cable ferrule with a pair of soft-nosed pliers; with the other hand revolve the twist-grip sleeve to the closed position, thread the nipple end of the wire into the head and slowly rotate the sleeve when the housing will locate the nipple; when located, replace the thimble over the wire and screw into the head.

Dismantling (1945–55 Model TR5). *Head Clamp Screws.* Take the two halves of the head away after removing the two screws.

Rotor Sleeve. Disconnect the cable nipple and withdraw the sleeve (4, Fig. 69) from the handlebar.

Assembly (1945–55 Model TR5). *Rotor Sleeve.* Grease the handlebar and slide on the sleeve.

Throttle Cable. Fit the wire nipple to the rotor sleeve.

Head. Assemble the two halves to the handlebar and rotor sleeve. Enter the clamp screws, position the cable guide tube into the recessed part of the twist-grip halves, and fully tighten the two clamp screws.

ENGINE REMOVAL (1945-59)

The removal of the engine from the frame may at rare intervals be required in order to effect a major overhaul in your garage (if you have one) or at a

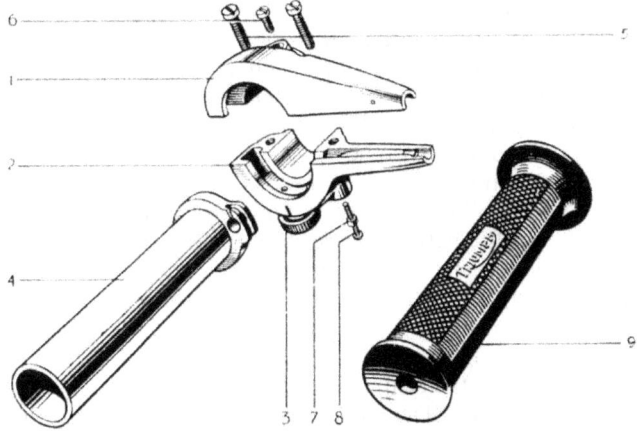

FIG. 69. TWIST-GRIP (1945-55 MODEL TR5)

1. Head assembly, plain half
2. Head assembly, threaded half
3. Friction adjuster screw
4. Sleeve
5. Head clamp screw
6. Grub screw
7. Locknut
8. Stop screw
9. Rubber grip

Triumph repair workshop. The engine and gearbox are separate units on all 1945-59 models, except on models 3TA and 5TA, which have a combined engine and gear unit. The following instructions give an outline of the procedure required for removing the engine or engine and gear unit, as the case may be.

Rigid Frame Models. Remove the twinseat (more commonly referred to as the dualseat). On a model fitted with a saddle remove the front bolt and tie the saddle back. Turn off both petrol taps, disconnect the petrol pipes, unscrew the four bolts which secure the petrol tank, and remove the tank.

Remove both exhaust pipes and silencers. On models 5T and 6T each exhaust pipe and silencer can be removed as a unit; loosen the finned clip bolt and the bolt securing the silencer to the frame. On model TR5 the exhaust pipes are freed from the cylinder head by unscrewing the adaptors with the "C" spanner provided in the tool kit. Slacken off the branch clip bolt and remove the silencer bolt. The exhaust system can now be removed.

On models 5T and 6T remove the nuts which secure the torque stays to the cylinder head bolts and slacken off the stays to frame bolt. The torque stays may then be disconnected. The steady on model TR5 utilizes a front engine bolt through a clip which is fitted to the lower tank rail. Remove the bolt to disengage.

Disconnect the cables for the throttle and magneto (model TR5 only) at the handlebars, and disconnect the cable for the air lever (models 5T and TR5 only) at the rear stays. Loop the cables neatly and as closely as possible to their respective engine fittings.

Remove the near-side footrest and detach the off-side footrest and spindle by merely withdrawing them. Also unscrew the spindle nut for the rear brake pedal and remove the pedal.

It is necessary to remove the primary chaincase, alternator (where fitted), the clutch, and the engine sprocket. Also disconnect the battery leads and remove the battery carrier-clip bolt. The battery can then be removed. Remove the battery carrier top nut and the two base bolts; the battery carrier and the air cleaner can then be released. Unscrew the rear chainguard to chaincase bolt and withdraw the chaincase from the shafts.

Lay a drip-tray beneath the engine and disconnect the engine supply and return pipes at the crankcase, and also the rocker oil feed pipe at the rocker-box spindles. Remove the terminal wires from the dynamo and the domed nut on the timing cover. Slacken the clip screw and withdraw the dynamo.

Insert a strong box of suitable height beneath the crankcase so that the sump plate rests on it. Remove all the front engine plates, studs, and nuts, except the lower front one. Then deal with the rear engine plates. Remove the two front top studs and nuts, and slacken the remainder. Tilt the engine towards the rear of the motor-cycle and swing forward the front engine plate. The engine can then be lifted out of the frame.

"Swinging Arm" Models (Except 3TA and 5TA). Remove the front and loosen the rear securing bolts. Then detach the twinseat or dualseat. Turn off both petrol taps, disconnect the petrol pipes, unscrew the four bolts securing the petrol tank, and remove the tank.

Remove the exhaust pipe and silencer assemblies by loosening the finned clip bolts and removing the bracket and silencer bolts. Slacken the frame lug bolt, unscrew the torque stay to engine bolt nuts, and remove the torque stays from the engine.

Disconnect the throttle and magneto (where fitted) cables at the handlebars, and the air lever cable from the off-side of the handlebars (models TR5 and TR6) or at the rear frame stays (other models). Neatly loop the cables as close as possible to their respective engine fitting.

Remove both footrests, but leave the spindle in position. Take out the split-pin which secures the operating rod to the rear brake pedal and then unscrew the pedal spindle nut and withdraw the pedal after disengaging the stop-lamp switch spring.

GENERAL MAINTENANCE: THE ENGINE

Remove the primary chaincase, the alternator (where fitted), the clutch, and the engine sprocket. Place a suitable drip-tray beneath the engine and disconnect the engine oil pipes at the crankcase, and the rocker feed pipes at the rocker-box spindles. Remove the terminal wires from the dynamo (where fitted), and also the dome nut on the timing cover.

Place a strong box of suitable height under the crankcase so that the engine sump plate rests on it. Remove the nuts from the two upper studs. The studs can then be driven out and the cover plate removed. Where a dynamo is fitted, slacken the dynamo clip screw and withdraw the dynamo from its housing. Remove the remaining studs to release the front engine plates. With regard to the rear engine plates, it is only necessary to deal with the engine plates to crankcase studs. Remove the two top studs and nuts, and slacken off the nuts which secure the lower stud.

Remove the box from beneath the crankcase and tilt the engine towards the rear of the motor-cycle. The lower crankcase stud will then disengage itself from the engine plates. Now lift the engine out of the frame housing.

Models 3TA and 5TA. The engine/gear unit can be removed from the frame in the following manner. Slacken the bolts in the finned exhaust clips, remove the small bolts which secure the exhaust pipes to the lower stays, and remove the silencer hanger bolts. Each exhaust pipe and silencer can then be removed as an assembly.

Remove the bolt and nut which secure each footrest and jar the footrests free of the taper mounting. Remove the nut on the rear brake pedal spindle, and the split-pin and washer. Then lift off the rear brake pedal. Remove the connecting link and detach the secondary chain.

Remove the air filter connexion. Detach the petrol pipe at the tap, unscrew the fixing nuts, and the mixing chamber cap ring. Then withdraw the carburettor. The throttle slide will still be attached to the throttle cable and should be secured in a safe place. Take off the insulating block which is fitted between the carburettor and the inlet manifold, and put it in a safe place.

Detach the clutch cable at the handlebar lever and coil it neatly at the gearbox. Detach the coil lead (centre cable) from the distributor, and detach the low tension wire. Pull these wires clear of the cable sheath. Disconnect the alternator cable at the snap connector beneath the gearbox.

Remove the engine torque stays. Remove the acorn nuts and long bolts which secure the oil feed pipes to the rocker-box. Disconnect the oil pipes at the rubber connectors below the oil tank.

Remove the bottom engine stud and distance pieces, support the engine on a suitable box, and then remove the front engine plates completely. Remove the front and top rear studs from the engine rear plates, and swing the plates up and backwards. The complete engine/gear unit can then be removed.

APPENDIX

SUMMARY OF MAINTENANCE AFTER RUNNING-IN

	Approximate Maintenance Periods	
Engine	*Miles*	*Kilometres*
Check oil level in tank and replenish if necessary.	250	400
Drain oil tank when warm and re-fill.	1,500	2,500
Clean oil tank and crankcase filters.	1,500	2,500
Check and adjust valve clearances	3,000–4,000	5,000–6,000
Clean and adjust sparking plugs	2,500	4,000–5,000
Decarbonize and top overhaul.	10,000–12,000	15,000–18,000
Gearbox		
Check oil level and replenish	1,000	1,500
Drain oil (when warm) and re-fill	5,000	8,000
Check tightness of clamp nuts.	1,000	1,500
Primary-chaincase		
Drain oil and re-fill (if 1,000 miles is not covered, change monthly)	1,000	1,500
Check cover security screws	1,000	1,500
Forks		
Drain oil and re-fill	5,000	8,000
Renew bushes, bearings and oil seals.	20,000	30,000
Steering Head		
Apply grease to lower head race	1,000	1,500
Check play in head races.	5,000	8,000
Re-pack head races with grease	10,000	15,000
Swinging Arm		
Apply grease with gun	1,500	2,500
Wheels (Rigid)		
Re-pack with grease	10,000	15,000
Check wheel bearings for play.	2,000–3,000	4,000–5,000

	Approximate Maintenance Periods	
	Miles	*Kilometres*
Wheels (Spring)		
Re-pack with grease	20,000	30,000
Check wheel bearings for play	5,000	8,000
Chains		
Adjust tension if necessary*	1,000	1,500
Lubricate secondary chain whenever necessary.		
Brakes		
Grease cable and rod mechanism	1,000	1,500
Adjust (normal running)	1,000	1,500
Grease brake cam spindles	1,000	1,500
Battery		
Check level of acid solution and add distilled water to bring level above plates monthly. In very hot weather check more frequently.		
Tyre Pressures		
Check and where necessary correct weekly.		
Carburettor		
Dismantle and clean	1,500	2,500
Air Filter		
Clean and re-oil filter element. (The servicing period should be at more frequent intervals where the machine is used under very dusty conditions.)	2,000	3,000
Change filter element	10,000	15,000
Magneto		
Check contact-breaker gap	2,000–3,000	4,000–5,000
Lubricate cam felt with thin oil	3,000	8,000
Grease rocker shaft with petroleum jelly	3,000	8,000

* No adjustment is necessary for the primary chain of Models 3TA, 5TA.

	Approximate Maintenance Periods	
	Miles	*Kilometres*
Distributor		
Check contact-breaker gap	3,000	5,000
Lubricate cam and pivot post with thin grease or oil.	5,000	8,000
Lubricate automatic timing control with thin machine oil	5,000	8,000
General		
Lubricate all cables and handlebar levers; check all nuts and bolts	1,000	1,500

INDEX

AIR filter, 22–4
Alternator, 49–52
Amal carburettor—
 maintenance, 18–22
 tuning, 15–18
Ammeter, 45
Automatic voltage control, 44, 45

BATTERY maintenance, 59–61
Brake adjustment, 78–80

CABLES, H.T., renewing, 49
Carbon, removing, 111
Carburettor—
 functioning, 11–15
 maintenance, 18–22
 tuning, 15–18, 24
Chain—
 adjustment, 82–4
 repairs, 86
Chains, cleaning, 84–5
Chromium, cleaning, 67
Cleaning, 66
Clutch—
 adjustment, 89–90
 dismantling, 90–2
Commutator, 46
 brushes, 45
Connecting-rod and crankshaft assembly, 119
Contact-breaker gap, 48, 52, 55
Contacts, cleaning, 48
Control cables, adjusting, 3
Controls, lay-out of, 3–5
Cylinder block—
 refitting, 119
 removal, 114
Cylinder head removal, 102–6, 108–9

DECARBONIZING, 101–111
Distributor, cleaning, 52, 54
Dry sump system, 28–30

EMERGENCY starting, 50
Enamel, cleaning, 66

Engine—
 oils, 41
 removal, 123–6
Engine and gearbox, cleaning, 66

FILTERS, 40
Focusing headlamp, 56
Front forks, 68–70
Fuel consumption, excessive, 18

GAP—
 contact-breaker, 48, 52, 55
 piston ring, 116
 sparking plug, 62
Gearbox maintenance, 89
Girling suspension damper units, 88
Grease nipples, 37
Greases, suitable, 41

HEADLAMP, 44, 49, 56–9
High-tension cables, 49, 56
Horn, 61
Hydrometer, Lucas, 60

IGNITION, coil, 52
Ignition timing, 97–101

LIGHTING switch, 44
Lubricants, 41, 43
Lubrication—
 brake, 38
 changing oil, 38–42
 clutch, 38
 contact-breaker, 52, 54
 controls, 38
 dynamo, 45
 engine, 30–3
 gearbox, 33, 42
 magneto, 46
 primary chaincase, 36, 41
 secondary chain, 37
 steering head, 38

OIL tank, replenishing, 38
Oils, changing, 38–42

PETROL tap—
　adjustment, 27
　positions, 6
Pick-up, high-tension, 49
Pilot jet obstructed, 17
Piston—
　removal, 117–9
　rings, 114–6
Preliminaries, 1

RECTIFIER, Lucas, 52
Running-in, 7

SIDECAR hints, 88
Slow-running, bad, 17
Sparking plugs—
　cleaning, 63–4
　suitable, 62
Specific gravity, 60
Starting, 6, 7
Starting trouble, 65

Steering, 9
Steering head, 70
Stopping, 9
S.U. carburettor, 24–7
Synchronizing twin carburettors, 17
"Swinging arm" frame, 87

TAKING over machine, 2
Topping-up battery, 59
Twist-grip, 121
Tyre pressures, 80–1

VALVE—
　clearances, 93–5
　guides, 113
　springs, 112
　timing, 95–7
Valves, removing, 112

WHEEL removal, 72–8
Wiring diagrams, 47–53

AUTOBOOKS WORKSHOP MANUALS

ALFA ROMEO GIULIA 1300, 1600, 1750, 2000 1962-1978 WSM
BMW 1600 1966-1973 WSM
BMW 2000 & 2002 1966-1976 WSM
BMW 2500, 2800, 3.0 & 3.3 1968-1977 WSM
BMW 316, 320, 320i 1975-1977 WSM
BMW 518, 520, 520i 1973-1981 WSM
FIAT 1100, 1100D, 1100R & 1200 1957-1969 WSM
FIAT 124 1966-1974 WSM
FIAT 124 SPORT 1966-1975 WSM
FIAT 125 & 125 SPECIAL 1967-1973 WSM
FIAT 126, 126L, 126 DV, 126/650 & 126/650 DV 1972-1982 WSM
FIAT 127 SALOON, SPECIAL & SPORT, 900, 1050 1971-1981 WSM
FIAT 128 1969-1982 WSM
FIAT 1300, 1500 1961-1967 WSM
FIAT 131 MIRAFIORI 1975-1982 WSM
FIAT 132 1972-1982 WSM
FIAT 500 1957-1973 WSM
FIAT 600, 600D & MULTIPLA 1955-1969 WSM
FIAT 850 1964-1972 WSM
JAGUAR E-TYPE 1961-1972 WSM
JAGUAR MK 1, 2 1955-1969 WSM
JAGUAR S TYPE, 420 1963-1968 WSM
JAGUAR XK 120, 140, 150 MK 7, 8, 9 1948-1961 WSM
LAND ROVER 1, 2 1948-1961 WSM
MERCEDES-BENZ 190 1959-1968 WSM
MERCEDES-BENZ 220/8 1968-1972 WSM
MERCEDES-BENZ 220B 1959-1965 WSM
MERCEDES-BENZ 230 1963-1968 WSM
MERCEDES-BENZ 250 1968-1972 WSM
MERCEDES-BENZ 280 1968-1972 WSM
MG MIDGET TA-TF 1936-1955 WSM
MINI 1959-1980 WSM
MORRIS MINOR 1952-1971 WSM
PEUGEOT 404 1960-1975 WSM
PORSCHE 911 1964-1973 WSM
PORSCHE 911 1970-1977 WSM
RENAULT 16 1965-1979 WSM
RENAULT 8, 10, 1100 1962-1971 WSM
ROVER 3500, 3500S 1968-1976 WSM
SUNBEAM RAPIER, ALPINE 1955-1965 WSM
TRIUMPH SPITFIRE, GT6, VITESSE 1962-1968 WSM
TRIUMPH TR2, TR3, TR3A 1952-1962 WSM
TRIUMPH TR4, TR4A 1961-1967 WSM
VOLKSWAGEN BEETLE 1968-1977 WSM

VELOCEPRESS AUTOMOBILE BOOKS & MANUALS

ABARTH BUYERS GUIDE
AUSTIN-HEALEY 6-CYLINDER WSM
AUSTIN-HEALEY SPRITE & MG MIDGET 1958-1971 WSM
BMW 600 LIMOUSINE FACTORY WSM
BMW 600 LIMOUSINE OWNERS HAND BOOK & SERVICE MANUAL
BMW ISETTA FACTORY WSM
BOOK OF THE CARRERA PANAMERICANA - MEXICAN ROAD RACE
COMPLETE CATALOG OF JAPANESE MOTOR VEHICLES
CORVAIR 1960-1969 OWNERS WORKSHOP MANUAL
CORVETTE V8 1955-1962 OWNERS WORKSHOP MANUAL
DIALED IN - THE JAN OPPERMAN STORY
FERRARI 250/GT SERVICE AND MAINTENANCE
FERRARI 308 SERIES BUYER'S AND OWNER'S GUIDE
FERRARI BERLINETTA LUSSO
FERRARI BROCHURES AND SALES LITERATURE 1946-1967
FERRARI BROCHURES AND SALES LITERATURE 1968-1989
FERRARI GUIDE TO PERFORMANCE
FERRARI OPP, MAINTENANCE & SERVICE H/BOOKS 1948-1963
FERRARI OWNER'S HANDBOOK
FERRARI SERIAL NUMBERS PART I - ODD NUMBERS TO 21399
FERRARI SERIAL NUMBERS PART II - EVEN NUMBERS TO 1050
FERRARI SPYDER CALIFORNIA
FERRARI TUNING TIPS & MAINTENANCE TECHNIQUES
HENRY'S FABULOUS MODEL "A" FORD
HOW TO BUILD A FIBERGLASS CAR
HOW TO BUILD A RACING CAR
HOW TO RESTORE THE MODEL 'A' FORD
IF HEMINGWAY HAD WRITTEN A RACING NOVEL
JAGUAR E-TYPE 3.8 & 4.2 WSM
LE MANS 24 (THE BOOK THAT THE FILM WAS BASED ON)
MASERATI BROCHURES AND SALES LITERATURE
MASERATI OWNER'S HANDBOOK
METROPOLITAN FACTORY WSM
MGA & MGB OWNERS HANDBOOK & WSM
OBERT'S FIAT GUIDE
PERFORMANCE TUNING THE SUNBEAM TIGER
PORSCHE 356 1948-1965 WSM
PORSCHE 912 WSM
SOUPING THE VOLKSWAGEN
TRIUMPH TR2, TR3, TR4 1953-1965 WSM
TUNING FOR SPEED (P.E. IRVING)
VEDA ORR'S NEW REVISED HOT ROD PICTORIAL
VOLKSWAGEN TRANSPORTER, TRUCKS, STATION WAGONS WSM
VOLVO 1944-1968 ALL MODELS WSM
WEBER CARBURETORS (EMPHASIS ON ALFA & FIAT)

BROOKLANDS BOOKS & ROAD TEST PORTFOLIOS (RTP)

AC CARS 1904-2009
ALFA ROMEO 1920-1933 ROAD TEST PORTFOLIO
ALFA ROMEO 1934-1940 ROAD TEST PORTFOLIO
BRABHAM RALT HONDA THE RON TAURANAC STORY
BUGATTI TYPE 10 TO TYPE 40 ROAD TEST PORTFOLIO
BUGATTI TYPE 10 TO TYPE 251 ROAD TEST PORTFOLIO
BUGATTI TYPE 41 TO TYPE 55 ROAD TEST PORTFOLIO
BUGATTI TYPE 57 TO TYPE 251 ROAD TEST PORTFOLIO
DELAHAYE ROAD TEST PORTFOLIO
FERRARI ROAD CARS 1946-1956 ROAD TEST PORTFOLIO
FIAT 500 1936-1972 ROAD TEST PORTFOLIO
FIAT DINO ROAD TEST PORTFOLIO
HISPANO SUIZA ROAD TEST PORTFOLIO
HONDA ST1100/ST1300 PAN EUROPEAN 1990-2002 RTP
JAGUAR MK1 & MK2 ROAD TEST PORTFOLIO
LOTUS CORTINA ROAD TEST PORTFOLIO
MV AGUSTA F4 750 & 1000 1997-2007 ROAD TEST PORTFOLIO
TATRA CARS ROAD TEST PORTFOLIO

VELOCEPRESS MOTORCYCLE BOOKS & MANUALS

AJS SINGLES & TWINS 250cc THRU 1000cc 1932-1948 (BOOK OF)
AJS SINGLES 1955-65 350cc & 500cc (BOOK OF)
AJS SINGLES 1945-60 350cc & 500cc MODELS 16 & 18 (BOOK OF)
ARIEL 1939-1960 4 STROKE SINGLES (BOOK OF)
ARIEL LEADER & ARROW 1958-1964 (BOOK OF)
ARIEL MOTORCYCLES 1933-1951 WSM
ARIEL PREWAR MODELS 1932-1939 (BOOK OF)
BMW M/CYCLES R26 R27 (1956-1967) FACTORY WSM
BMW M/CYCLES R50 R50S R60 R69S (1955-1969) FACTORY WSM
BSA BANTAM (BOOK OF)
BSA ALL FOUR-STROKE SINGLES & V-TWINS 1936-1952 (BOOK OF)
BSA OHV & SV SINGLES - 250cc 1954-1970 (BOOK OF)
BSA OHV & SV SINGLES 1945-54 250-600cc (BOOK OF)
BSA OHV SINGLES 350 & 500cc 1955-1967 (BOOK OF)
BSA PRE-WAR MODELS TO 1939 (BOOK OF)
BSA TWINS 1948-1962 (BOOK OF)
BSA TWINS 1962-1969 (SECOND BOOK OF)
CATALOG OF BRITISH MOTORCYCLES (1951 MODELS)
DOUGLAS PRE-WAR ALL MODELS 1929-1939 (BOOK OF)
DOUGLAS POST-WAR ALL MODELS 1948-1957 FACTORY WSM
DUCATI 160cc, 250cc & 350cc OHC MODELS FACTORY WSM
HONDA 50 ALL MODELS UP TO 1970 INC MONKEY & TRAIL (BOOK OF)
HONDA 90 ALL MODELS UP TO 1966 (BOOK OF)
HONDA MOTORCYCLES 125-150 TWINS C/CS/CB/CA WSM
HONDA MOTORCYCLES 250-305 TWINS C/CS/CB WSM
HONDA MOTORCYCLES C100 SUPER CUB WSM
HONDA MOTORCYCLES C110 SPORT CUB 1962-1969 WSM
HONDA TWINS & SINGLES 50cc THRU 305cc 1960-1966 (BOOK OF)
HONDA TWINS ALL MODELS 125cc THRU 450cc UP TO 1968 (BOOK OF)
INDIAN PONYBIKE, BOY RACER & PAPOOSE ILL PARTS LIST & SALES LIT
J.A.P. ENGINES 1927-1952 & MOTORCYCLES 1934-1952 (BOOK OF)
LAMBRETTA ALL 125 & 150cc MODELS 1947-1957 (BOOK OF)
LAMBRETTA LI & TV MODELS 1957-1970 (SECOND BOOK OF)
MATCHLESS 350 & 500cc SINGLES 1945-1956 (BOOK OF)
MATCHLESS 350 & 500cc SINGLES 1955-1966 (BOOK OF)
NORTON 1932-1947 (BOOK OF)
NORTON 1938-1956 (BOOK OF)
NORTON DOMINATOR TWINS 1955-1965 (BOOK OF)
NORTON MODELS 19, 50 & ES2 1955-1963 (BOOK OF)
NORTON MOTORCYCLES 1957-1970 FACTORY WSM
NORTON PREWAR MODELS 1932-1939 (BOOK OF)
NSU PRIMA ALL MODELS 1956-1964 (BOOK OF)
NSU QUICKLY ALL MODELS 1953-1963 (BOOK OF)
RALEIGH MOPEDS 1960-1969 (BOOK OF)
ROYAL ENFIELD SINGLES & V TWINS 1937-1953 (BOOK OF)
ROYAL ENFIELD SINGLES 1946-1962 (BOOK OF)
ROYAL ENFIELD 736cc INTERCEPTOR FACTORY WSM
ROYAL ENFIELD 250cc & 350cc SINGLES 1958-1966 (SECOND BOOK OF)
SUNBEAM MOTORCYCLES 1928-1939 (BOOK OF)
SUNBEAM S7 & S8 1946-1957 (BOOK OF)
SUZUKI 50cc & 80cc UP TO 1966 (BOOK OF)
SUZUKI T10 1963-1967 FACTORY WSM
SUZUKI T20 & T200 1965-1969 FACTORY WSM
TRIUMPH PRE-WAR MOTORCYCLE 1935-1939 (BOOK OF)
TRIUMPH MOTORCYCLES 1937-1951 WSM
TRIUMPH MOTORCYCLES 1945-1955 FACTORY WSM
TRIUMPH TWINS 1945-1958 (BOOK OF)
TRIUMPH TWINS 1956-1969 (BOOK OF)
VELOCETTE ALL SINGLES & TWINS 1925-1970 (BOOK OF)
VESPA 1951-1961 (BOOK OF)
VESPA 125 & 150cc & GS MODELS 1955-1963 (SECOND BOOK OF)
VESPA 90, 125 & 150cc 1963-1972 (THIRD BOOK OF)
VESPA GS & SS 1955-1968 (BOOK OF)
VILLIERS ENGINE (BOOK OF)
VINCENT MOTORCYCLES 1935-1955 WSM

PLEASE VISIT OUR WEBSITE
www.VelocePress.com
FOR A DETAILED DESCRIPTION
OF ANY OF THESE TITLES

Please check our website:

www.VelocePress.com

for a complete up-to-date list of available titles

www.ingramcontent.com/pod-product-compliance
Lightning Source LLC
Chambersburg PA
CBHW070554170426
43201CB00012B/1834